Cultivate Your Calling

Even in Crisis, Men Can Walk in Their True Identity, Discover Purpose & Monetize Their Gift

By Lionel Hilaire

Praises for *Cultivate Your Calling*

"This is a well-needed book to encourage and strengthen any man at any stage who wants to be a powerful example and walk courageously."

- Arlene Williams

"It revealed some things to me about myself that I never considered in the past and I'm confident that it will do the same for the men who take the time and digest this content with an open mind."

- Jimmie Williams, JW Acquisitions & Development

"In this book Lionel is transparent and open. If you truly apply the principles covered in this book, I believe it will bring freedom in areas such as properly identifying your role as a man in the lives of others, understanding your God given purpose, and seeing yourself how God sees you."

- Luke Jones, Jones Luxury Real Estate Group

"Cultivate Your Calling addresses one of the least talked about subjects of our time; namely, the mental well-being of young men. While the role of men in our society is changing, Lionel here, goes against the national narrative-du-jour by encouraging men to find their calling and become precisely what God created them to be. This is a must read for young men, old men, and the women who love them."

- -William Honore, Owner/President of Florida Tax Deed Liquidation Trust

"Many men are afraid to have these conversations, but this book will definitely help them gain the confidence to do so."

- Wilky Cajuste, CajusteConsulting & Co

"Cultivate Your Calling is not just for men. It can help ladies to understand men. This book will help men to understand themselves and they are not alone with their feelings and emotions...It's ok to open up to become that LION."

- Donna Jarrett-Mays, ADJ Financial Services, Inc

Praises for *Cultivate Your Calling*

"This book is going to definitely impact and change men's lives and in the same token women are going to receive an understanding as to why men are the way they are and how we can truly help them to develop into their potential."

- Dr. Shamonia Wimberly, The Success Strategist
Founder of the Success Strategist Institute

Praises for *Cultivate Your Calling*

Dedication

This book is dedicated in the memory of Tyrell Thrower, my daughter Kyla's late boyfriend. Although his death is unfortunate, it gave life to this book that was on the inside of me this whole time. Because of him, I've been motivated to help males repivot and grow from boys to men.

After more than two years of Tyrell dating Kyla, I began to accept him as my son-in-law. So much so, I wanted to build a bond with him so I could help assure he was the best man he could be for my young lady. He didn't need much

Dedication to *Tyrell Thrower*

improvement. Tyrell had a plan, a vision, and great love for my daughter.

I remember how Kyla would talk about them getting married. In her mind, she was planning a wedding, but in reality, Kyla planned a funeral.

It's hard to look at his photo and accept that he is no longer with us. On the day of his burial, as we walked away from his lowered casket, I hugged Kyla and assured her that he would never be forgotten.

Men across the world will know Tyrell's name, and it will outlive the short 21 years he spent on this earth. I am thankful to him for taking great care of Kyla. She has blossomed greatly, and I'm so proud of her.

I promise to help our men discover and maximize their potential, so they don't have to feel like they need to pick up a gun and take a life. #JusticeForTyrellThrower

Dedication to *Tyrell Thrower*

Tyrell Thrower

October 16,1998 – March 29,2020

Dedication to *Tyrell Thrower*

Thanks

To my beautiful children Kyla, Chelsea, Syleena, and Lionel Jr.

You four have been so instrumental in my life. It's a privilege and an honor to be your father. Daddy loves you.

To my wife, Sierra. I could write pages of gratitude. Thanks for 15 plus years of marriage. Thanks for helping me with the title of this book. Thank you for being patient and putting up with me all these years! I don't want to know where I would be without you. You are definitely suitable for me, thanks!

Contents

Foreword

Once in a while, a new book comes out that really impacts a generation. In his new book *Cultivate Your Calling*, Lionel Hilaire meticulously lays out the evolution of moving from boyhood to manhood. This in-depth examination of the challenges, failures, mistakes, and triumphs of men goes to the heart of what many need to understand about real transformation. Men in general are bombarded by so many influencing forces, but most black men face difficult obstacles from the moment they arrive on this planet.

The task of being a community champion, a faithful husband, a hero for your children, and a role model for others is most times overwhelming and causes a lot of men to shrink into less impactful roles. With the help of this book,, men will be able to reflect and reset in their quest to be the best that they can be.

In my time of knowing Lionel, I have been impressed by his strong and unwavering desire to educate and empower men. I commend Lionel for this book, which is another effort by him and a tool to strengthen our manhood. I celebrate Lionel as a true champion for the cause of helping men live out their manhood in a successful and inspiring way. This book is a must-read!

-Allen B. Jackson

Pastor and Author of *The Freedom of Forgiveness*

"Unforgiveness will empower those who owe you to own you."

Preface

I wrote this book because I strongly believe that if the man who murdered Tyrell Thrower understood and cultivated his calling, he would not have taken his life. I'm also writing this book because a book like this would've enabled me to prepare for manhood when I was a teenage father, in my marriage, my community, and in my career. Writing this book helps me to give back to males that remind me of myself.

I believe if a man recognizes why he exists, he will be less likely to take his own life. According to Well Space Health[1], in 2014, 80% of suicides amongst African Americans were males (United States). In the same research, it shares that Caribbean Black men in the U.S. have the highest

---

[1] www.wellspacehealth.org

suicide attempt rate in the African American community.

As you might understand, this is a very sensitive topic to write about and personal to many—including myself after such a tragedy in my family. However, when I look at Tyrell's photo every time I log on my computer to write this book, and each time I have flashbacks of my then 18-year-old daughter leaning on my chest to cry out as we left the burial site, I know I must write and publish this book. When I see all the men and boys that remind me of myself whose lives were taken over senseless crimes, and when I look at my own son Lionel Jr., I think to myself *"I must and will complete this book and leave all I have in it!"*

It is my opinion that you will find this as an on-time read and enjoy every page because intent and passion fill the pages. I wrote this book with you in mind. This is a valuable read for you because I share a stigma that has been placed on you. One you might have unknowingly placed on yourself that gets neglected by just about everyone around you, including you. Understanding the false identity that was given to you—plus more of what you will learn in this book—has the potential to help you transform your life in ways you only imagined.

In such times as we are in today, I am qualified to share this with you because, like so many other men, I have experienced various challenges like suicidal thoughts, systemic racism, workplace discrimination, police harassment, false accusations, mental health challenges, neglect from my parents, verbal and physical abuse. I persevered through it all and now I am a thriving person and an effective husband and father. I am a community leader with accolades such as Parent Leadership and Resident Leadership certification. Currently, I sit on the Social Services board in my city. I am Treasurer of Divine Potential Services, Inc., 501©(3) where over the last few years, we have helped hundreds of families come together to connect with mental health therapists, marriage and relationship experts, financial experts, and leaders and pastors in our community.

Now is the perfect time to pick up this book, read, and apply what you learn because times, as you see it, are tougher. Most of your life, you may have seen fatherless homes or abusive and dysfunctional men rampant in your community. Statistically, you are to follow in these men's footsteps and/or repeat the cycle until you're locked up or even worse.

This book provides you with the information you need to walk in your true identity. Discover your purpose and monetize your gift!

Cultivate the Call

The greatest enemy of the Black male is not crime, the "man," women, unemployment, the economy, or the President of the United States. The greatest enemy of a Black male is himself. The failure to live in his purpose destroys the Black man. He must obey his calling and have knowledge of self. You didn't choose to be a male, but you can choose to become a man.

You become a man when you cultivate the call on your life. For many males, this is the #1 problem. Being born a male but struggling to become a man. There are three key areas in a man's life he must cultivate in order for him to be who God intended him to be: his personal life, his relationships, and his career.

We Don't Know Where to Start

The greatest discovery in life is self-discovery. Until you find yourself, you will always be someone else. Be yourself.

- Myles Munroe.

Through the decades, trends, fashion, and music changed. Similarly, people also changed. Industries generated billions of dollars. Why? Because no one wants to feel left out or left behind. So, they become what they see—someone else. The journey to self-discovery is challenging but being someone else is even worse. I remember when I started the sixth grade. I was raised in a home where swearing was not allowed. At the start of middle school, I was the only one who didn't swear amongst my friends. Then I had an idea. I'll just remove the first letter or the first few letters in the cuss words, and I'll fit right in. No one will notice. That lasted a few days until one of my friends noticed and embarrassed me in front of everyone. It felt humiliating and that was not a feeling I ever wanted to experience again. Immediately after, I included every letter plus more in cuss words!

Later in life, I realized that so many other males experience similar identity crises. I felt like I lost myself. I didn't know who I was or why I was here on earth. I asked myself, "What's my life's purpose?" That's when I began my journey to discover my purpose-to lead, not follow.

After reading books and having different experiences, I began to witness a new man being born. I realized that most men I watched growing up looked great on the outside, but their marriages, careers, and—even worse—their identities deteriorated on the inside; I made up my mind not to live like that anymore. After all, who wants to look like a public success but be a private hot mess? Many of us men struggle with who we were meant to become, and many of us men don't know where to start to rectify the disconnection. The first step is to acknowledge the struggle. Acknowledging that I was following the wrong people, trends, and other things was essential to my transformation from boy to man.

We all Have Potential But...

According to Google, potential means *"having or showing the capacity to become or develop into something in the future."*

My definition of potential is *something great within you that is not yet seen on the outside. Original intent. What you could do but have not done yet. A gift you possess that needs to be shared with your tribe (the people you were called to serve). Maybe, hopefully, and possibly.*

We all have potential, but potential alone isn't good enough. You must understand, release, and maximize your potential. Not operating in your purpose goes against the reason for your existence. For me, not living my life's purpose led to anger, frustration, loneliness, and low self-worth. When I found my life's purpose, it helped me heal from brokenness, and I developed the confidence to lead and find clarity along the way.

My life had more meaning, and it felt great to wake up in the morning to take on the day. In *Cultivate Your Calling*, you have the solution right in your hands, so you don't have to repeat this cycle ever again! The cycle of internal chaos. Uncertainty, self-doubt, low self-esteem, codependency, ruined relationships, instability in your career, etc.

You have a gift to share with the world. Otherwise, we will continue to have girls and boys grow up lost, broken, angry, bitter, broken, and contagious because they refused or neglected to lead and share their gift with others. So, on the behalf of myself and the people you are called to serve… GIVE ME MY STUFF! Read this paragraph again, and dive into this book today!

Section One

Cultivate Your Identity

Chapter 1

Men Are Not Dogs. We're Lions

Women, "Why do men cheat?"

When I thought about writing this book, I became very excited. I was thrilled because I had discovered some things about myself, and perhaps about many men, that are worth sharing. I joined a challenge that I found on Facebook that helped me write this book. It was a tremendous feeling. I felt like I was going to complete this book in no time.

I began the challenge, turned in my homework daily, and I even began to write the table of contents and how I wanted to outline the entire book. On the fifth day, I began to encounter some resistance (many call it writer's block).

I didn't know what to write. I wrote an entire chapter, but I had to erase it and start over again. I heard voices haunting me saying, "Who do you think you are? You're not qualified to talk about men. You're not qualified to help men." I knew right away this book must be written. This book must be composed because there are so many books out there that inaccurately write about men, and there are even some books out there by famous and popular people that do not represent men accurately.

Are men really dogs?

Man Is the Only Creature Who Refuses to Be What He Is.

- Albert Camus

I remember standing in the club and other events packed with men in attendance. A man with a mic would ask, *"Where's my dogs at?!"* Then a shout with deep voices would erupt, *"Roof, roof, roof, roof!!"* Mimicking dogs. Being a little boy who aspired to become a man one day, I admired every minute of it and was looking forward to shouting the same with my deep voice one day.

Years later, I recall doing the same thing. It felt incredible at the time. Any boy who is amongst men mimics those men. Men don't like to feel left out. We prefer to be a part of a brotherhood. You know we are tight when we say, *"Hey, what's up dog?"* This was a very common thing in the 90s and early 2000s and still today.

When you look at it, men have been behaving exactly how they identify one another—as dogs. I purchased a book written by a well-known celebrity thinking I was going to get some awesome advice on how to be a more effective male, like how to create a healthy, balanced life as a man. Mistakes to avoid in relationships and how to position myself to have a thriving career. The way this guy did so much press about the book, I thought I already knew what the book was about. I was looking forward to key pointers for this book that could help me and other men.

I did some research on the book so I could gain some more clarity about this chapter. However, when I read the table of contents, I began to turn my head in disappointment. The introduction and five chapters referred to men as dogs. I thought to myself, "This can't be good."

Women hate that men act like dogs. So, I logged on Amazon to read the reviews. Oh, how right was I! There were dozens of reviews saying the author wrote the word dog so much in the book, they had to put it down because they basically became sick of the book and felt as if they wasted their money.

Even some men felt it was degrading. I thought again to myself, "Why would this man write a book like this?" I'm not knocking this author, nor am I mad at him. He may have written the book from his heart. He wasn't raised by his father, so that makes me more compassionate towards him. He wanted to help men the best way he knew how.

However, I've read at least thirty to forty of these reviews, and I learned that women hate when men refer to themselves as dogs. There were over 400 reviews. I'm sure hundreds, if not thousands of women read this book.

I was thinking about the behaviors of a dog. It just didn't make sense to me why men are compared to dogs. Some dogs eat their own poop. Male dogs mate with any female dog he can find, have puppies, and move on to the next dog. Most dogs bark, but don't bite. Some dogs protect, some run. Don't get me wrong, dogs can make great pets for therapy companionship, but men cannot be compared to dogs. The breed is inconsistent.

One day I had an epiphany. Then it made sense to me why many men act like dogs. We were trained to believe we are dogs, so we act like dogs.

So, is this why men cheat?

Women across the world want to know the answer to this very question. To my surprise, even some men want to know. I haven't done my research, but I'm sure this is a billion-dollar question/business.

Here's my answer. My answer may shock you. Now, I'm not a licensed therapist. I'm a high school and college dropout. Right after being kicked out of high school, I applied for a homeschool diploma. I passed the test by cheating. I share this with you just in case you thought I was some big shot, super educated person. Nope! I'm not.

But let's get to the point. Why do we mistreat our lovely ladies? What causes us to sever their hearts and abandon them like waste on the curb, waiting to be picked up by the man in the beat-up truck?

To be truthful, I'm not as concerned about that question. Nope. Not really. I believe there's something more or equally significant to ask. That question is what is the root cause of dysfunctional men?

See, I don't know every man who has betrayed their lady. So therefore, I'm not qualified to answer that question. I would do a disservice if I attempted to be everyone's hero and explain with my own theory of why men cheat.

Although it's horrible what men have done to our women, we must converse about something that needs greater attention. Like I mentioned earlier, we must get to the root cause. I'll share mine shortly. Asking why men cheat might be a legit thing. It may assist us to correct the problem, but we can certainly see it really hasn't helped us much.

Personally, I know why I cheated. I know why after 11 years of marriage, I stepped out. It was by far the worst decision I made in my entire life. None of what I mention here should be taken as an excuse but should instead help you avoid making the same mistakes.

This still hurts a bit to share, but I must. I didn't plan on sharing this with you in detail, but I believe you need to know.

Years ago, my wife was experiencing some pains in her body. I think she had a few doctor visits, but they could not tell her what was wrong. The pain was heavy on her. I felt bad. I felt like I couldn't help the love of my life. She would have convulsions.

The pain Sierra was experiencing was so great and happened so often that I didn't know what to do. I contacted a few friends of hers to send her some words of encouragement, but they didn't. I'm sure they didn't know what to do or say. In fact, I think only one of them knew about her situation. Her very close friend up north.

This went on for so long that I began to have a great desire for sex because we weren't active while she was suffering of course. How was I going to ask her for sex? Like, how was I going to say, "Hey honey, I know you're in a lot of pain, but I want some." So, I didn't bother to ask. Instead, I began to feel some type of way. Feelings of loneliness, abandonment, rejection, and neglect surfaced.

On a Sunday, as I was driving to work, I can recall feeling bad for my wife and crying hysterically. This might sound crazy, but when I think about it, I believe I was crying for two reasons: my wife in pain and not being able to help her and this strange voidness and brokenness within me. Almost like a crackhead who can't get a hit! Seriously, but more about that in a bit.

I got to work and began to do my job like every other day. But I was broken on the inside. I wouldn't wish my emotions at that time on anybody. It's a feeling that can't be explained. Half the day went by, and one of my customers who had been doing business with me for years came in for her appointment to have her vehicle repaired. She wasn't a regular customer like many others I had. Her and I had conversations here and there on the phone before. I felt something unusual about her, but I couldn't put two and two together.

Like I did for most of my customers, I had her vehicle ready in no time, but she decided to stay until closing. I locked the store and told her how tired I was and that I needed to get a massage. She offered, so I accepted. We decided for her to follow me to a nearby parking lot. On my way there, I heard a voice say, "You need to drive straight home and cancel the massage with this lady." I continued to drive and thought nothing would happen since I was dirty and we were just chilling.

We got to the parking lot and she sat in the backseat of my car. About a minute later, I joined her in the back. We spoke for a few minutes and we began talking about sex. I made a comment to her about oral sex and she offered to do it, so I let her.

Right after that, I thought to myself, "Was it worth it and what was I thinking?" But it was too late. The damage was already done! That same week, I was scheduled to preach at our beta church service. Yup. I was playing the role of a pastor.

I couldn't speak without hearing voices of condemnation saying, "God has stripped you of your anointing!" Over and over. And because of self-doubt and repeated condemning thoughts, things didn't go well, so we shut it down after the third service. I'm glad it ended that way. I never wanted to be that type of leader.

A few months later, I told my wife what I had done. It broke her heart, but somehow, someway, she forgave me. My wife told me she knew something wasn't right with me lately. Trust me, I hated what I had done. It was also strange that she forgave me—almost like God told her about it before I did.

It's amazing because all the previous times I'd done anything to break her trust it would take a while for her to forgive me. It took her awhile to conduct herself like our relationship was back to normal. However, just because she forgave me doesn't mean that my trust was automatically earned. That nonetheless needed to occur.

Lust and Addiction

This feeling of me feenin' like a crackhead was so weird! I tell a story about the details of discovering me having symptoms of codependency in my first book *How to Rescue Yourself from Rescuing Others, 7 Steps to Getting Healthy, Happy and Healed.* The complete story and other stories about my addiction, pain, and sufferings and how I overcame them (and how I am still overcoming them) are also included.

Codependency is like having a dependence on something like drugs and sex, but this type is a dependence on a person. Here is the google definition:

co·de·pend·en·cy

/ˌkōdəˈpendənsē/

Noun: Excessive emotional or psychological reliance on a partner, typically one who requires support on account of an illness or addiction.

Brokenness and False Identity

I've experienced so much as a boy and a teen that manifested as dysfunctional behavior and toxic desires. From being bullied, neglected, rejected, beat up, picked on, ignored, etc., leading me to desire attention at all costs. Like desiring for sex early in life. I had sex and smoked marijuana for the first time at fifteen. There's a saying: *"Boys rather go in the wrong direction than go nowhere at all."*

Because my father worked around the clock, came home, ate dinner, and went straight to bed right after, I looked to my friends and rap music to show me what life is like and how to become a man. Like many Black boys, my identity was established in what I was taught by my friends and the music we listened to. The music and my friends taught me to slap a woman if she gets out of line and to have multiple sex partners. (That was over twenty years ago. Imagine how much worse music has gotten.)

I clicked with a peer in ninth grade. I'll call him John. This kid was so intelligent and well-spoken. I liked that about him, so we stuck together. In tenth grade, I received my permit to drive. Remember, John was a well-spoken guy. He was also bold and could get the phone number to almost every girl he talked to.

John's phone list grew. So much so, I got tired of taking him to meet up with girls in my mom's car without having a date myself. I let John know that I wasn't taking him to see girls if she didn't have a friend for me to date. From that day forward, we dated and had sex with plenty of girls. This is what we did from ages fifteen to eighteen.

How many times have you heard someone say, *"I say whatever's on my mind!"* or *"I keep it 100."* That was me years ago. To me, that's like indirectly admitting that a person is unable to control his emotions. There's no way a man can cultivate the call on his life being emotionally unstable. We must acknowledge our pains, deal with them by seeking counseling from professionals, read the right books, understand what the Bible says about your emotions, learn to heal from them, and repeat these steps every time we experience trials that challenge our peace.

There's no healthy and effective way you can keep it *100* all the time. If you find yourself having to do that often with the people around you, it might be time for you to do inventory of your surroundings. This book was written to help you have discipline in your personal life, your relationships, and your career. Lack of emotional IQ leads to dysfunction in these areas.

Lust Is Idolatry and Says, "I Want More!"

That was just a snapshot of what we did from ages fifteen to eighteen. Our desire for sex grew. We met girls that would allow a group of us boys to have sex with them at one time. We called these sex acts "trains." The Urban Dictionary accurately writes it: "An activity usually involving *multiple* males and *one female.*"

We would have girls our age or older women to perform these acts. Google defines lust as a *"very strong sexual desire."* Lust is not just sex-related, but for the sake of this topic, we will only be covering sex here.

*Colossians 3:5: Put to death
therefore what is earthly in you:
sexual immorality, impurity, passion,
evil desire, and covetousness, which
is idolatry.*

After having so many of these sexual desires and encounters, lust grew and grew in my heart. I thought the sexual cravings I had was a "man thing." But it was a lust thing. *Lust does not discriminate. It can take you places you never intended to go and keep you longer than you planned to stay.* For example, many men struggle with porn addiction. Porn addiction is a billion-dollar industry and unfortunately, it's growing. Because lust is a strong desire for a person or thing, the Bible defines it as idolatry.

*Exodus 34:14: "For thou shalt
worship no other god: for the LORD,
whose name is Jealous, is a jealous
God."*

If you are single and you battle with lust, I encourage you to get help before entering a relationship. If you are married or in a relationship and you struggle with lust, I strongly suggest you get the support you need. Why? Because I thought getting married would resolve my strong appetite for sex and I thought lust for my wife was a good thing, as long as I didn't have it for someone else. However, that was a deception I fell for.

Proverbs 27:20 (MSG): Hell has a voracious appetite, and lust just never quits.

Lust says, "I want more!" That's when men dive into things like hanging out at the strip club, watching porn (which is known to destroy relationships), eyeing other women, starting conversations with them, and eventually adultery and/or fornication.

For me, lust, brokenness, addiction, false identity, poor decision making, and denial led me to make the biggest mistake of my entire life. I was hard on myself for a long time. Lust, brokenness, addiction, and a false identity can cause you to make decisions that can hurt you and others.

Some Solutions

When I left the life of a *player,* I had no idea I was still fighting with lust. Even though I left the physical lifestyle, it was still in my mind. For years I was told to be strong and use will power, and lust desires will go away.

I realized that it wasn't true in the worst way possible. I truly believe in prayer but dealing with and healing from lust requires more than prayer. After all, we are spiritual *and* natural beings.

Yes, you should pray, but also get the help you need, like making an appointment with an expert, reading books like this and/or seeing a therapist. Make certain you do your own research. Another thing I want to recommend is fasting. Intermittent fasting is my favorite. Oftentimes, I go 21 days without eating past 6pm or 7pm. I only drink water or unsweetened tea after those hours. During those times, pray and read scriptures about lust or whatever you struggle with.

One thing I learned is that I must specialize in myself according to God's Word. My mental, physical, emotional, relational, and financial health are my priority. This means to focus on yourself as it relates to these areas. When restoring or setting a foundation for your life, it all begins with the internal work in the areas mentioned above. Specialists help to give clarity and support, but you must do your homework.

> *Galatians 1:26: But I say, walk habitually in the [Holy] Spirit [seek Him and be responsive to His guidance], and then you will certainly not carry out the desire of the sinful nature [which responds impulsively without regard for God and His precepts].*

We all need the Holy Spirit's guidance, so we do not fulfill our own lustful ambitions. Before Jesus left His disciples. John 14:26

> *But the Helper (Comforter, Advocate, Intercessor—Counselor, Strengthener, Standby), the Holy Spirit, whom the Father will send in My name [in My place, to represent Me and act on My behalf], He will teach you all things. And He will help you remember everything that I have told you. - AMP*

The Comforter, Advocate, Intercessor—Counselor, Strengthener, Standby. Yes. When I read that scripture, I was like, come on! Christ wants to be our everything. It's okay to listen to advice from people whom you admire, but these people should conform with what the Holy Spirit is telling you. Don't take advice from people that only speak to your *flesh* (ungodly self).

For example, you just moved into your home and you need furniture, so you ask a friend if you should pay cash or rent-to-own because you don't want to look like you're broke. A "yes man" or "yes woman" friend would say, "Go ahead and rent-to-own." A real friend would say, "Naw, brah, wait until you can pay for it all. Don't worry about what people think."

Brain fog is the inability to have a sharp memory or to lack a sharp focus. I didn't feel like myself, and I wasn't able to think clearly. Ignorance led me to make decisions I regretted. After scheduling an appointment with my doctor, I found out that my testosterone levels were extremely low, and my estrogen levels were a bit higher than they should be.

Quickly, I knew this could not be good. Not only was I broken, but I was deficient. I was in bad shape mentally and physically. I remember suffering from heavy brain fog. My thoughts were rarely clear, and this caused me to be edgy and frustrated most of the time. Any minor disagreement triggered me to be angry and say things I shouldn't say.

Walk in Sobriety

Today, I'm in the best mental state I've ever been in and I feel great most days. I love to consume content by Dr. Daniel Amen and Dr. Caroline Leaf. Look these two up; I promise you won't regret it. Dr. Daniel Amen's supplements helped me recover from brain fog.

Taking supplements, going on bike rides, drinking plenty of water, and playing basketball again makes me feel good. My marriage is thriving. Sierra and I guide couples and empower youth through our nonprofit organization Divine Potential Services Inc. Visit our Facebook page to see all the beautiful pictures of families in our community whom we inspire and empower.

1 Peter 5:8: Be sober [well balanced
and self-disciplined], be alert and

cautious at all times. That enemy of
yours, the devil, prowls around like a
roaring lion [fiercely hungry], seeking
someone to devour.

It is virtually impossible for any man to be effective in his life when he is not in his right mind. Being sober is not exclusive to alcohol. Drunkenness is not only being influenced by alcohol and drugs. It includes secular elements like music, entertainers, TV shows, trends, and more. Typically, when you aren't taking care of yourself, you are easily manipulated out of God's will for your life.

When was the last time you went to the doctor? Have you been checked for deficiencies or illnesses? Are you taking supplements that your body needs? How do you maintain reasonable health? If you have not been to the doctor recently, I encourage you to make an appointment and get some blood work done to find out what areas in your health you should address. Also, ask your doctor what daily multivitamin he or she recommends.

Read, read, and read. Read your Bible. In today's times, seek God's ways more than ever before making decisions about your health or other life decisions. Look up scriptures related to your health as needed. If you haven't already, I challenge you to make that doctor's appointment ASAP. Get your testosterone levels checked. My doctor explained to me that after age thirty, men's testosterone levels begin to decrease. He recommended I take vitamin D3. Now I take the vitamin, and I make sure I'm in the sun so my skin can absorb vitamin D as well.

In the next chapter, I want to share something that requires your undivided attention. You must be present and alert to get what I'm going to share with you. If you must read the next chapter twice, please do so. I'm serious.

Not only for yourself but for the people banking on you to become the man you were created to be. You were created on purpose, for a purpose, by God. You were made in His image, after His likeness (Genesis 1:26), so God's reputation is on the line every time you take on the day.

So again, take great care of your health, physically and mentally. More on that later. But for now, here is a summary of this chapter:

- Lust does not discriminate. It can take you places you never intended to go and keep you longer than you planned to stay.

- Women hate when men refer to themselves as dogs.

- Dogs make great pets, but not great men.

- You were created on purpose, for a purpose, by God.

Next, you will discover how to denounce the dog.

Chapter 2

How to Denounce the Dog Mentality Without Feeling Like You've Lost Yourself

---

"What you focus on expands. So, focus on what you want, not what you do not want."

-Esther Jno-Charles

Would you agree that the worst thing in the world is feeling like you've lost yourself and that your hands are tied behind your back? It was about three years ago when I found myself lost—feeling like my hands were bound behind my back.

I was the cofounder of our new nonprofit organization. We were hosting its first family conference. So many lives were touched in a nearly sold-out event. I had just discovered what I wanted to do for the rest of my life, which is to uplift and inspire others and help them have newfound faith. But at that time, it was Lionel who needed the inspiration he gave to others. My whole life, I assumed leaders and superheroes don't bend or break. (I guess it's because I watched too many cartoons growing up!) They are deemed to be the "strong ones." Others depend on them to carry everyone to the finish line. They should never do anything wrong or ever reveal their weaknesses. This was an ongoing conversation in my head since middle school. I believed every word of it. I had experienced some of the worst days of my manhood. My wife was ill, and I was experiencing brain fog at the same time. There was no one I could think of who I could just call to ask for help or guidance. It's like something had taken over my mind and body. My emotions were all over the place. This might have been the worst and the lowest point of my life. The thoughts of regret, feelings of resentment, fear, anxiety, depression, anger, and frustration only intensified.

It Was All Fake!

Remember in chapter one when I learned that I was suffering from codependency? I was angry, bitter, confused, and felt naked, taken advantage of, and lonely all at once.

I felt like every minute up to that moment was fake. I believed the relationships and deals were fake too. I felt like my entire life was fake. Why? Because most of the things I did for those around me was to please them. It was so they would accept me. The upper hand was always theirs and because of that, I wanted to change my life and make things work my way. What I didn't understand was that I had to set healthy boundaries. If someone asked for a favor from me and I had a need, I must make sure to share what I expect from the other person as well. I had to make sure it was mutually beneficial.

When I was nearly thirty years old, I had suicidal thoughts. There were loud voices in my head. It sounded like someone was speaking to me out loud. Because I never dealt with this experience, I cultivated the spirit of fear. The spirit of fear manifested into voices urging me to take my life. I became overprotective of my wife and children because I thought something might happen to them. For example, if my wife or one of the children developed a fever, I would immediately panic and think to myself, "What if he or she dies?" These weren't casual thoughts, by the way. Because I became so anxious, I would purchase all types of medicines, natural herbs, and binge on reading articles. Then I would *report* my findings to them and make everything seem life threatening! Later, everyone in the house would avoid conversations and time with me because of this.

What saved my life (and my family) was the Scriptures I learned from the Bible, the desire for growth and change, and the love I have for my wife and children. I strongly believe that brokenness from trauma like emotional neglect, physical, sexual, and verbal abuse, etc., can cause and/or create fear, lust, rejection, and rebellion if it's not dealt with right away. Brother, I don't want this to be you, because demonic spirits like these can wreak havoc in your life. For example, sexual abuse at a young age that goes untreated or unresolved is known to increase the likelihood of things like homosexuality, fornication, pedophilia, plus more.

Many of us don't like to share what we are feeling or going through. We'll look at our doctors/therapists in the eye and tell him/her about our issues at work and at home, but we won't share what's going on within. Men often think that strength and time will heal our issues.

We also don't want to be perceived as crazy or weak, so we keep our issues to ourselves—only for them to show up in areas of our lives that affect not only us but our families.

Here are some statistics from The Centers for Disease Control and Prevention:

• In 2017, the suicide rate for men was 3.5 times higher than it was for women.

• Men over the age of 65 are at the greatest risk of suicide.

• Research also suggests that while women attempt suicide more often, men choose more lethal means of suicide, like shooting or hanging themselves.

These are some alarming statistics. Black men are absent from millions of homes in America due to incarceration, homicide, heart disease, etc. Mental health is something we must discuss, and that's one reason why I wrote this book. It's to help empower you to be the man God intended you to be. I share these stats so you understand how vital your mental health is. When your mental health is compromised, you can make disastrous decisions that you regret.

Denounce the Dog

Here are a few ways to denounce the dog mentality so you don't have to go down a painful path of uncertainty. I want you to be clear about who you are. The dog mentality is not what this book is all about, but it's where I believe we must begin because of the narrative and reputation of the Black male.

Rebuild

Jesus answered, "Destroy this temple and I will build it again in three days." - John 2:19

If you know anything about construction, you know that a house can be in its worst shape, but if the foundation isn't damaged, you can repair the home. However, if the foundation is damaged or even cracked, the whole house must come down.

It's promising that your rebuilding isn't physical, it's spiritual, and that's the temple Jesus is referring to. You must allow Him to have His way and make you new again. One major way to allow Christ to have His way is to surrender.

> *Come to me, all who labor and are heavy laden, and I will give you rest. Take my yoke upon you, and learn from me, for I am gentle and lowly in heart, and you will find rest for your souls. For my yoke is easy, and my burden is light.*
>
> *- Matthew 11:28-30*

He said, "I will give you rest!" Sex, money, and drugs are usually what we do to *release* or feel *high*, but these things only provide temporary relief. After you have sex, get money, and do drugs, you will most likely feel worse than when you began.

Oftentimes, you may have to surrender more than once. It's like peeling back layers of an onion. After a few peels, however, you might begin to feel better about discovering things about yourself.

Some things that you thought you overcame were just suppressed.

It's bittersweet to find areas in your mind that God doesn't have territory in. It's bitter because you didn't know you gave birth to challenges this deep. It's sweet because it's an opportunity for growth and restoration.

Don't Care

The fear of man lays a snare, but whoever trusts in the Lord is safe.

-Proverbs 29:25

No matter how much you do, or how great you do it, there is always at least that one person who will look at you like you stepped in poop. They *ain't* never satisfied with anything that's attached to you. If you attain something you've worked hard for, they'll be the last to congratulate you, if at all. This person would try to make you feel unaccomplished no matter what. You'll be joyful then out of nowhere, here comes *Negative Nathan* or *Debbie Downer*. You know a person like this. It's hard to accept there's someone like that in your life, be it family or friends—they just can't give you props when it's due. You must accept it and keep it moving. Even if it's somebody very close to you. Don't pay attention to the opinions of others that do not add value to your life. You'll never be able to please everyone and that's okay.

Over the years, I've encouraged people to step out and do something great for themselves and others by sharing their story. Instead of doing it, walking by faith, they would ask, *"Do you know what people are going to think?"* I would let them know that there will always be the few that'll have something negative to say no matter what and that their story can be a blessing to someone else. I'd have them think about their own lives and ask, "Think back on your life. Is there at least one person whose story inspired you? If they kept their story to themselves because of what others might think of them, how much would you have missed out? The same way, if you don't share your story, many will suffer.

I came to be more confident in myself after not caring about the negative things people say about me or my family. It wasn't easy for me to get there because I was a people pleaser. Codependency made me value people more than God. Only your heavenly Father should have this kind of influence over you that compels you to examine yourself based on His Word and not another man or woman's word or opinion.

Take Care

According to Black Demographics[2] **the number one cause of death for African Americans is heart disease**. Self-care is the best remedy you can implement. To ensure you are in the best health possible, take time out of your day to go for a thirty-minute walk or however much time you can without getting dehydrated. Pick an activity that works best for you. I enjoy going on thirty-minute bike rides daily and playing basketball on Sundays. It is a great start to my day. Bike rides in the morning help filter my thoughts and allows me to reflect. I love it! If I don't take my bike ride in the morning, my day feels like it's thrown off. Bike rides may not be something you like or have the convenience to do. Find an activity that makes you feel good. Some people do their activity in the morning and some do their activity in the afternoon; choose the time of day that works best for you.

Please do not say you don't have time. You must prioritize your schedule by utilizing the calendar on your phone. God has given us a great desire to have a sense of fulfillment when we work, take

---

[2] https://blackdemographics.com/health-2/health/

care of our families, and do the things He has called us to do. I used to give from an empty cup. I experienced plenty of brain fog from past head injuries. When I began to take my supplements, have some quiet time alone, pray, reflect, and research how to be more effective with self-care, my thoughts became clearer. My mood was much better, and I became more excited about life.

Talk to Yourself

Many people like to focus on their external challenges. They blame everybody and their momma for their troubles.

Here are two quotes that sum this up:

If you blame everyone for you being where you are today, then you're admitting that they are the only ones who can fix your problems. -Lionel Hilaire

It's not your fault, but it's your responsibility. -Will Smith

Maybe it's not your fault that you are at rock bottom, but it's your responsibility to heal, be restored, and begin the journey to cultivate your calling. I understand we get hurt by the people we least expect to hurt us. However, what I've learned is that the greatest revenge in life is success. Constantly thinking about how terrible someone treated you only holds you back from moving forward in your life. It's like carrying heavy weight that's not yours. Talk about baggage.

Death and life are in the power of the tongue, and those who love it will eat its fruits.

- *Proverbs 18:21*

Say this with me: *"I no longer believe nor desire to be like a dog. I am created in the image of and after the likeness of God. I affirm myself today as a man. A new man. I was born a male, and now I'm a man. No longer will I treat myself and others in the degrading ways I used to. I believe and receive eternal joy, restored relationships, and prosperity in my life. I'm a new man now. If I ever compare my ways to an animal, it will not be a dog... it's a lion! Now I am prepared to cultivate my calling."*

Remember this: inner conversations determine your behavior and your actions. So speak life and think positive. How? By first being mindful of what you allow to enter the gates of your heart (Proverbs 4:23).

Talk to Dad

Most importantly, talk to God. Every morning, I pray *The Lord's Prayer* (Matthew 6:9-14). I believe it covers every area of my life. I've learned that prayer is allotting God permission to intervene on earth. How awesome is that?

When you pray, you are giving God earthly authority to work on your behalf and on the behalf of others. Whatever you need Him to do, just pray in Jesus' name. When you pray in Jesus' name, you are praying to activate everything Jesus stands for: peace, love, joy, healing, deliverance, protection, victory, provision, prosperity, binding, and loosing. I've heard people pray curses on others, but that's not what Christ stands for. I don't believe that type of prayer will go higher than the ceiling. Plus, that might be witchcraft.

You should never pray for someone's downfall. Oftentimes, people are not evil, they're just broken. And *broken people break people.* You should pray for their healing and deliverance instead. However, you don't have to remain in the presence of a person who drains you. When you pray, you are in essence saying, "I surrender my own way and my own will." Prayer is a true indication of humility. It shows yourself and God that you don't have all the answers and you rely on the One who does... God.

Do You

I learned that there is good selfishness. When I began to overcome codependency, I had this idea to take myself to the movies. This felt so weird to me at first because I've never gone to the movies by myself. However, it was a great experience. It was nice to watch a movie in the theater, enjoying my own popcorn.

Do you plan to do something nice for yourself? When was the last time you went out to eat as a treat for yourself? How long has it been since you sat in total silence, smiled, and had positive thoughts?

Stop right now and write a little about that thing you haven't done for yourself in a while.

_____

_____

_____

_____

_____

_____

_____

How does that make you feel? (Be honest)

_____

_____

_____

_____

_____

_____

_____

What date have you taken yourself on this month? If you haven't yet, what will it be?

_____

_____

_____

_____

_____

_____

_____

Think about it and express how you feel. Smile or say a loud yes! How does that make you feel now that you have it planned?

_____

_____

_____

_____

_____

_____

_____

So, you see, there is such a thing as good selfishness. Planning to do for yourself after you have taken care of your family and worked hard during the week is a sign of a healthy life balance.

Be Consistent

God compares Himself to a lion several times throughout the Bible (Jeremiah 25:38 & 50:44, Hosea 11:10 & 13:7).

Therefore, I chose to compare men to lions. Not all dogs are brave, but all lions are brave. Not all dogs fight, but every lion will. Not all male dogs protect their babies, but male lions won't let you come close to their cubs. This leads me to believe that men were never meant to be like dogs; we're more like lions. Lions are consistent.

Lastly, I want to share this poem I wrote in less than an hour. What I put together for you feels like this was directly off the press in Heaven. Have you ever seen that neon light at Krispy Kreme that reads, "Hot Now"? That's exactly how I felt when this poem downloaded to my mind!

Lionel Hilaire

Here it is:

New Man Poem

Now I must admit, I was wrong

Thought I was a dog all along

There was help out there, but it missed me

So, I began to search for someone to fix me

My identity was slandered, I was treated like dirt

Looking for a fix, so I chased skirts

Woman after woman, that didn't work

Pretending I'm strong, but I'm really hurt

You couldn't hear my moaning, 'cause it was silent

They say men don't cry, so I became violent

Later I found out that I've been lied to

And I've been tricked since junior high school

See, change came after I stopped trying

I realized...I'm just like a lion

All this time, I let him use me

But right now, the Devil gotta loose me

I'm no longer that same man

Cause I put my life in God's hands

So, brother, let me tell you this

There's no such thing as a quick fix

So, denounce the dog, it's not who you are

You've been made in the image of God

Now look up to mount Zion

You went from a dog and now you're a lion!

There's nothing else really that can truly explain my past better than the words you just read! I hope this was a blessing to you as it was for me. I hope that you enjoyed it. If you did, please let me know. Post it and tag me on social media. I can be found under Lionel Hilaire. Thanks in advance.

Here's what we covered so far:

- If the foundation is damaged or even cracked, the whole house must come down.

- You'll never be able to please everyone and that's okay.
- Your subconscious mind doesn't sleep. It works around the clock and delivers according to the thoughts you deposit in your mind.
- There is such a thing as good selfishness.
- Men were never meant to be like dogs... we're like lions.

The next chapter will be one you won't forget. We are going to review what I call **"The L.I.O.N. Assessment."** I want to make sure this book lands in the hands of at least 100,000 men to greatly impact their lives so they can do the same for their families and others.

***

Before we proceed, I want to ask you for your honest opinion. Go to Amazon.com and leave a review of what you like best so far from what you have read in this book. You can also visit my Facebook business page at Facebook.com/LionelHilaireSpeaks and leave a review as well. This would be a great gift to me if you could do that for me and fellow readers. Thanks.

Chapter 3

Discover and Cultivate Your L.I.O.N.

---

*A purpose does not just happen, it
is cultivated.*

- Unknown

Since you're reading this book, I will be transparent with you. This is the only way I can be as effective. When I wrote this book, I was on a journey to comprehend and explore. At times, it didn't feel good. At other times, I was excited and felt like I could take on the world.

Google.com defines *calling* as *a strong urge toward a particular way of life or career, a vocation.* Synonyms include *mission, summons, profession, occupation, pursuit, and walk of life.*

If you have not yet discovered your calling, don't worry, we will go over that later. However, you get to have an upper hand with **"The L.I.O.N. Assessment."** If you have already discovered your calling, then this may help you become more effective in all areas of your life.

Let's get started with the foundation of your calling. The foundation is below the ground. It supports us throughout life. Let's explore what it means to cultivate. There are two meanings, according to Google.

For this book, we'll explore the second definition: *try to acquire or develop (a quality, sentiment, or skill)*. Synonyms include *till, plow, dig, turn, work, prepare, pursue, and foster.*

This was God's command for the man in Genesis 2:15 (AMP) before He presented a woman to the man. Before you try to impress a woman, you must be cultivated first. As Adam was cultivating, God said in Genesis 2:18, *"It is not good for the man to be alone. I will make him a helper who is right for him."* (NCV)

Did you catch that? God saw the man working, pursuing, digging, and fostering, so He gave the man a **helper who was *right* for him**. I love that! Don't you? I love this because I can see how this scripture relates to my life. It was not until I began to cultivate that my marriage became more effective. My wife was always the right one for me, but it wasn't going to show until I began to cultivate. What do you think happens to the man who refuses to cultivate? *Even if* he finds a lady, he will not receive her properly because he is not tilling, plowing, digging, preparing, and pursuing.

The Breaking Point

One day, I was listening to TD Jakes speak, and he said something so profound that it stuck with me. Here's what he said:

> *"You will never do anything great until you can get past your breaking point."*

Those words woke me up when I heard them! What TD Jakes said really got my attention. I quickly looked back over my life and saw how many times I started something, then stopped. Started something again, then stopped. It was easy in the beginning. I'd tell everybody what I was doing. I would get so excited and call people up I hadn't called in a while and share my new venture.

But when things got tough, I would say to myself, *"I didn't sign up for all of this!"* I didn't think it was going to be this challenging. That excitement did not survive through difficulty, so I put my head down and turned around. See, I realized where my quitting mentality kicked in as I looked back. I would have this false sense of joy in the beginning, then say, *"God did it!"* But when challenges began to arise, I would quit prematurely.

I realized when I got past my first true breaking point. It was in my marriage. During the first few years, I couldn't see us go further than five years. We were constantly having disagreements. If my wife had a positive criticism about me, I would take it as if she were attacking me instead of as constructive feedback. The "D" word flew from my mouth so many times! Divorce was my go-to word because deep down, I thought that was a way to shut her up and force her to agree with me. Although it did silence her, I truly believe she was being wise. She knew that I was dealing with something I needed to overcome. She never mentioned divorce throughout our marriage. This shows you how toxic and controlling I was.

One day, I heard my former Pastor say that I must stop praying for my wife to change, but pray that I understand her better. Prior to hearing him say that, I thought my wife was the problem.

Although she had her shortcomings, I believe I had influence over her, and she looked up to me for guidance as a man and a husband. When my pastor shared that with me, I was certain that my prayers needed to shift. Never did I think that I had to change. That revelation not only helped me change my perspective, but it also helped me become wiser and more mature so I could learn how to overcome challenges that helped me get past my typical breaking points. Instead of projecting, I did more reflecting. Self-reflection.

How many things in your life have you launched but have not completed? Or you looked at a mountain and thought, *"That's too big!"* Instead of fighting past your fears and/or worries about it, you returned to your comfort zone. It's probably more than you can count; I know because it was the same for me. I had to learn why I turned away from hardships. Once you understand and get past your breaking point, things begin to fall into place. My marriage fell into place and we've been married since 2005; far past the five years I couldn't imagine.

The Obstacle Is the Way

Les Brown once said, *"If you live life easy now, then later, your life will be hard. But if you live life hard today, then your life will be easy later."*

I love this quote because it encourages me to get through tough challenges. It's easy to quit. It's so convenient to turn around, stand on a corner somewhere, and just chill with *the boys*. No matter what you are facing right now that makes you feel like quitting, always remember that what you need is on the other side of the obstacle. You must press through, face your fears and uncertainty. Yeah, it's a bit intimidating, but do it afraid. Think about it; if Michael Jordan simply walked away after being released from his high school basketball team, where would he be today? The game of basketball would have never been this great, and players would probably not be receiving such big contracts today. Yes, he faced a setback and may have thought about quitting, but he didn't. He pressed forward, changed the game of basketball and his family's legacy forever. For the record, I'm not a Chicago Bulls fan. I rep the Miami Heat. Go Heat!!!

There are some aspects in your life you might be giving too much thought to. That obstacle is blocking you from seeing what's really on the other side. The outcome is like a table spread of your favorite foods...just for you. However, you may be stuck focusing on the obstacle so you can't see the result.

On the other side of fear is success.

-Will Smith

Fear and faith work the same way. You never know what to expect. Why not have faith? Believe that you can tell that mountain to move and it shall move for you. You may be asking yourself why I am going on like this. It's because I'm prepping you for your breaking point. Every day you wake up and prep yourself for the day. You never know which day is going to test your breaking point the greatest. If you don't properly prepare for tests, trials, and tribulations, it will feel like your house was built on sand. Whenever the wind blows, the house falls. But if the house is on a solid foundation, then it will not be destroyed when the wind blows.

Prepare now so *when* tough challenges come your way, you are well equipped to face them head on. **The L.I.O.N. Assessment** is going to help you become well equipped and prepared. Let's get into it!

The L.I.O.N. Assessment

Have you ever done a self-assessment at work or in school? Well, this one is different. This assessment focuses on you, the person, not the employee or the student. Once you understand this concept, you can become a more productive person, employee/employer, husband, father, and student. Many people, including myself, always want to skip processes and head straight for success. Skip the process and life will spank you back to the foundation. Trust me, I know firsthand. For example, I remember when I launched a windshield repair business. I saw other people doing it, so I thought I should just attempt to do the same and business would take off.

However, I have never repaired a windshield a day in my life, but here I am with an LLC, a bank account, and tools with no real-life experience. Guess what happened to that business... it failed. I skipped the process of hands-on training, practicing, preparing, and went straight into business. The man who does not prepare, fails.

I made this assessment simple enough for a 5th grader. **The L.I.O.N. Assessment** can benefit you in your personal life and work and/or business. Before you begin, remember, if at any time you feel stuck, reach out to someone who knows you personally and has your best interest at heart to help you complete this as thoroughly as possible. If you have a wife or longtime girlfriend, she might be the best person to help you.

Legacy

Legacy is the memory and physical things you leave behind. For example, as it relates to memory, a legacy I have and I'll be remembered for is effective communication. This skill allows me to make meaningful connections and potentially land big deals. It also helps me properly handle conflict in my career, wherever I go and most importantly, at home with my wife and children. Do you see how critical this can be in your personal and professional life? Great.

I challenge you to take a few minutes to think of some strengths you have. This is where you have permission to brag about yourself a little.

What strengths do you possess that you can leverage to leave a positive legacy?

_____

_____

_____

_____

_____

_____

_____

How do you feel about having these strengths?

_____

_____

_____

_____

_____

_____

_____

How does it make you feel to see the legacies you're leaving behind?

_____

_____

_____

_____

_____

_____

_____

Insecurities

Everyone has something about themselves they feel uncertain of. For example, an insecurity I have is lack of traditional education, which tends to make me feel like I'm not good enough to lead.

What weaknesses are you struggling with that make you feel insecure?

_____

_____

_____

_____

_____

_____

_____

Think about what resources you can utilize to help you deal and overcome your insecurities. For example, learn a new skill by December.

What are they?

_____

_____

_____

_____

_____

_____

_____

Opportunities

An opportunity is a resource you have that can help you become more effective in your daily life. For example, I have friends who are licensed therapists. I can call them when I am dealing with something I can't figure out or comprehend on my own.

What opportunities are available to you that you can take advantage of?

_____

_____

_____

_____

_____

_____

_____

How soon do you plan to leverage your opportunities?

_____

_____

_____

_____

_____

_____

_____

_____

Needs

Needs are things you must have to protect you and your family, so you avoid a crisis and are able to get out of a crisis if need be. You might be struggling with potential threats to your everyday life.

For example, finances are a common struggle. If I don't manage my finances sufficiently, I can potentially lose my home, causing me and my family to become homeless. Yes, it's that serious. You must be brutally honest with yourself. Take a few minutes to think about your needs. Think of them as threats (it's usually something that has been an ongoing life challenge).

What are some threats in your life you must address?

_____

_____

_____

_____

_____

_____

Now that you have listed your needs, look back at your opportunities and see how you can leverage them so you can get the help you deserve. If you are aware of an opportunity that can help you, but you didn't list it in the opportunities section, go back and write it down, then take the necessary action to resolve your needs.

Remember at the beginning of the chapter we covered the meaning and synonyms of cultivate? In this assessment, we did some digging. The parts where you address your L.I.O.N. is when you begin to till, plow, turn, work, prepare, pursue, and foster. In other words, that's when you begin to cultivate.

Man, I am proud of what you have just accomplished! Do you know how many men have never done a personal assessment on themselves? I encourage you to revisit it. I also suggest that you write today's date on this page so when you revisit it, you can measure your growth. Some people do their assessments annually and some six months at a time. It's up to you how often you want to assess yourself. I suggest at least once per year.

I truly hope you learned from this chapter. It's a great pleasure to have the privilege to impart the information. It will help you transition to being a man. Here is what you should have learned in this chapter:

- Once you understand and get past your breaking point, things begin to fall into place.
- The obstacle is the way to success.
- How to discover and cultivate your L.I.O.N.

In the previous chapters, you learned how to set a solid foundation in your life. Without reading and understanding the three previous chapters you just read, it is almost impossible to effectively move forward in life. Why? Because you would be bypassing a process that every person should address. You also learned about false identity, denouncing that false identity, and discovering your L.I.O.N. (How to discover your strengths, weaknesses, opportunities, and threats.)

In the next chapter, we strategically dive into the family. An area I am greatly passionate about also. I was nineteen with my first child, twenty-three when I got married, and now I'm in my late thirties. I have overcome so many trials and tribulations. If you have a family or plan to have one soon, this chapter is a must-read for you.

For now, I would like to know what you liked most in this chapter. Post about it, then tag me on IG at Instagram.com/LionelHilaire_. I love to hear how much my readers are enjoying my content. I look forward to connecting with you.

Section Two

Cultivate Your Family

Chapter 4

The Top 3 Mistakes Men Make and How to Avoid Them!

I always thought it was me against the world, until I realized, it was me against me.

- Kendrick Lamar

No one is perfect and men are not robots. One thing I don't claim to be is an expert in men's behavior or psychology. However, I do know a few things about what not to do. I've made so many mistakes, I can write a book about them!

What I've found is all the mistakes' men make fall under at least three categories. If we can avoid these mistakes at all costs, we can prevent misfortune in our lives and in the lives of the people we love. Our families depend on us. They don't expect us to be perfect, they just want us to improve and do our best.

Please read carefully what I'm about to share with you. These next three elements are what I've witnessed our women and children weep about. They cause breakups in homes, long-term hurt, and traumatic behaviors in our children. How do I know? It's because I've made these missteps that still pain me today. Things I can't take back. Mistakes I'm still earning trust for as I type. However, if the suffering I've caused can be turned into prevention or gain, I'll take that. All I ask of you is that you take them seriously.

I truly believe that our mistakes can work to others' advantage. A true friend will always speak from a place of compassion, truth, and best interest. That's my goal right now.

Leverage

Our competitive nature makes us not ask for help. If you are a woman reading this book, you probably said *Amen!* In fact, my wife would be laughing right now. We get so competitive until it has a negative impact on us. It's great to be competitive on the basketball court or in a contest at work. But I think we confuse competition and pride. Pride says, *"I don't need help"* or *"I can do this myself."* A wise competitive person would leverage the help around him.

I get it. You want to try to figure things out on your own. I understand how you feel. I felt the same way. But here's what I've found—asking for help is a manly thing to do. I hated to ask for directions. It used to make me feel like I didn't know what I was doing in front of my wife and children. It's almost like I felt less than a man. I'd rather drive around in circles until I found my destination. Then I look back at my wife and kids, and they have this look on their faces because we're late and could've simply made it on time if I asked for help. They would've been impressed if I asked for help and got where we needed to go on time.

Another negligence can be found in our parenting. If we're having a conversation with another parent and they attempt to give advice, we say things like, *"I know. I'm a grown a** man.*

Don't tell me what to do with my kids. You take care of yours and I'll take care of mine."

Bro, it's not wrong for you not to know something. What's bad is pretending like you've got it all together. People see right through that. Your family respects you more when you ask for help. When things happen as they should, you're viewed as the hero. It shows that you care. Women and children don't think you're weak when you ask for assistance. They see it as strength when you get things done that save time, money, and energy.

Listen

When I was a child, I spoke as a child, I understood as a child, I thought as a child; but when I became a man, I put away childish things.

- 1 Corinthians 13:11

Listen with your eyes, not just with your ears.

-Unknown

I'm sure you watched *The Lion King* either as an adult or child. If not, shame on you! There are some very valuable life lessons in it, some of which I'll be talking about in this section. In the movie, when the lead character, Simba, was a cub, he was a bit hardheaded. His dad told him not to go to a certain place, but he did anyway. It wasn't until he experienced trials and made many mistakes that he realized his dad was right. As men, many of us don't learn from our faults as youths. We bring them with us in our adulthood.

I understand that certain circumstances are difficult. Like your dad not being active enough to nurture and cultivate you with critical life lessons. However, there comes a time in a man's life when he says, *"Enough! I have to take responsibility for my life, even though it's not my fault I didn't learn what I needed from my dad."*

Two Ears, One Mouth

Like you read earlier, self-talk is vital as long as you're not beating yourself up. One thing children hate is when we cut them off entirely when they're trying to explain their point. That's the fastest way for them to shut down for good.

You see, pride and the need to prove our manhood or masculinity are some of the reasons why we feel like we don't have to listen. Often, we feel as if we're losing or weak if the other person is right. That couldn't be further from the truth. You're not any less of a man if another person expresses themselves. You may have to apologize and/or make corrections and that is okay.

You're still a man even after you say, *"My bad, my fault"* or *"My apologies."*

You don't have to prove anything to anyone. It's okay to hear others out and be wrong at times. Listening, apologizing, taking out the trash, being told or asked to do something doesn't take away from you, it adds to your value.

Learn to listen to your family without interruption. Allow them to vent and respond with compassion, then cultivate where you see improvement is required.

Love

*So now faith, hope, and love abide,
these three; but the greatest of these
is love.*

- 1 Corinthians 13:13

One day, during the year 2007, my wife and I took our daughters to take photos. A guy walked up to me and asked if I wanted to buy some bootlegged DVDs. I quickly remembered the government was cracking down on piracy and I said, *"Naw, I'm good."* He walked over to Sierra and asked her the same thing. She says, *"You know you can go to jail selling those?"* If I am with my wife and/or children, I speak for our family unit. I had to brace myself for what could turn into an argument or worse. See, my wife, who I love dearly, has a way of telling strangers the truth because she is a caring person. When this happens, they become offended, which can cause an issue. A previous incident occurred with a 6'8" man. My 5'9" self-had to step in to defend my wife. It appeared I would have to do it again with the guy who had bootlegged DVDs.

They began to exchange words and there I was hoping that the dude would walk away. But no, they kept at it. I tried to play it cool because we had three little girls with us. Plus, I didn't want them to see daddy fight. I suddenly remembered that our former Pastor had just spoken about love and how we should practice it. I said I'm going to try exercising love because I'm learning how to free myself of that old mentality. I used to fight or get ready to fight when someone disrespected me or my family. Well, this might be the ideal time to try the "love" approach. So, I smoothly stepped in and said, *"Bro, all she trying to say is—"* He interrupted me with, *"N*** you broke, blah blah blah."* I don't remember exactly what he said after those few words, but I knew I had to think of something quick.

It's either fight or listen to my Pastor. What happened next was surprising. Never had I done this in my life. I said to him, *"Bro, you're smart. You don't have to do what you do. If you can burn CDs, imagine what else you can do."* He kept rambling on, but I kept imparting onto him. Finally, he walked away. Then I see him coming towards me a few minutes later.

By now, I'm ready to come out of the shirt! I didn't know what to think. In fact, I'm like, *"Pastor's advice didn't work!"* Plus, I haven't fought in a long time, what should I do? He comes up to me, extends his arm, shakes my hand, and apologizes to me. He then walked away, only to come back and shake my hand again! By now I'm thinking, *"This love stuff does work!"* A few weeks later, we saw the same man again and like our last encounter, he walked up to me and shook my hand.

Lesson Learned

At the end of the day, love wins. Quick disclaimer: it may not work right away all the time. But that time, it worked for me. Many other times, love worked. With my children being stubborn, love worked. With my wife nagging sometimes and saying the same annoying things over and over, love worked and still does.

It's a father's love, I believe, that our children and our families need above all else. Unconditional love. You can buy a huge house, brand new cars, all the latest toys and other fancy things, but those things can never replace the time and love of a father.

I worked sixty-plus hours a week in corporate America and it got me nowhere. You're nothing but a number to the world, but to your family, you're everything. They need time with dad. You might be thinking, *"I don't know what to say or what to do. I'm not that creative."* Your children desire your presence first.

To me, this by far is the #1 mistake men make: not expressing unconditional love for their families. We are too tough on our children. We are too aggressive at times with our women. A strong man to them is a vulnerable man. A man who expresses and shares his emotions with his family in a healthy way. They melt from that. I believe it's great for you and your family's mental health. I've put these practices to work in my own life and family. I know these statements to be true.

The story I shared with you earlier about the CD man was a turning point in my life. It confirmed to me that love works and that I needed it to work in my family. Before that moment, I used to treat our marriage like a business deal and as if we were roommates. I was always serious with a straight face when I would say to my wife, *"Sierra, we got bills to pay. We have lights, water, and a phone bill. I need everyone to listen to me and shut up!"*

I wasn't operating like a husband. I was functioning as a dictator. Never allow your family to feel anxiety in your home. Make your house a home by making it a place of security and affection. Everyone should be comfortable at home; they should want to come home and stay, not run away.

I wrote this book so you will not be negligent like Lionel Hilaire and millions of other men. Women and children came to me on many occasions expressing their love for their men, but not feeling loved in return. I believe you have what it takes to make a difference in your family's life.

The women I speak to say that their husbands act like they're no longer interested in their marriage, or they stopped dating because he got comfortable. These men get comfortable and gain weight. They stopped going out on simple dates. They are no longer buying flowers and gifts. We all know most women love gifts! I've seen beautiful homes split up because simple things are missing.

If you don't have children or a family but desire to, learn from my mistakes. I treated my home like a business and every employee was in trouble if things weren't right when I got home. Take this chapter as a learning lesson from me.

We covered quite a bit in this chapter. Here are some key things to take with you:

- Women and children don't think you're weak when you ask for help.
- Listen to your family without interruption. Allow them to vent and respond with compassion, then teach where you see improvement is necessary.
- Make your house a home by making it a place of security and affection. Everyone should want to run home.

In the next chapter, we are going into your bedroom (not literally).

Chapter 5

3 Ways to Ignite Passion in Your Marriage Without Counseling

The Lord God said, "It is not good for the man to be alone. I will make a helper suitable for him."

\-   *Genesis 2:18*

Dr. Myles Munroe once said, *"A helper must be as strong or stronger than the person they are helping."*

Cultivate Your Marriage

Please don't get it twisted, I'm not a therapist or anything like that. But my wife and I have sat down with enough couples to conclude that there are three main components a married man and woman must have to help ensure a long-lasting and healthy marriage.

For years, my wife and I lacked those components in our marriage. Has it been easy? No way. But it sure has been worth it. My wife and I always say that *if you want to develop quickly in life, get married, and make it work.*

I believe marriage brings out the best in you. But it can also bring the worst out of you if you don't give it your best, get married for the wrong reasons, or are prideful in your relationship. It takes two. However, it begins with you.

In this chapter, I'll share some things with you that have helped me and my wife stay married and enjoy it at the same time. These components helped me to cultivate my marriage in a positive and healthy way.

First Component: Communication

Communication to a relationship is like oxygen to life. Without it, it dies.

- *Tony Gaskins*

Communication alone isn't good enough. I believe effective communication is one major factor for your marriage to not only survive, but to thrive. Anyone can communicate, but not everyone knows how, or even cares to communicate effectively.

When Sierra and I were newlyweds, I would yell and get angry when I felt like she did not understand what I was trying to say or when she made a slick comment. To be honest, it went on like that for years. I thought yelling while using my deep voice would get attention and get kids moving. All it really did was give my wife and children anxiety. Attempting to make a person fear you by shouting is not a healthy practice. Studies show a person's self-esteem is lowered when they are constantly being yelled at.

Now, I make a great effort to remain calm when I speak to my wife when we disagree. I used to take what she said personally. I thought she was assaulting me and challenging my manhood. I finally realized once I stopped yelling that it was my insecurity speaking. However, because I'm a driven and passionate person, I tend to speak a little loud. I try my best to explain that I am not yelling, I'm passionate, then I lower my tone.

> *Do not let any unwholesome talk*
> *come out of your mouths, but only*
> *what is helpful for building others up*
> *according to their needs, that it may*
> *benefit those who listen.*
>
> *— Ephesians 4:29*

Even in a soft tone, certain words, like swearing and subliminal messages, are not effective forms of communication. Anyone who knows me knows that you might never hear me swear, but that doesn't matter if I belittle my wife when I speak. I must admit, I used to be a bit harsh to make my point when speaking to her.

Instead of being harsh with his words, women like when their husbands say nice things to them and communicate in a loving way. No wonder my wife was always turned off. Although I am the one who was more verbal in our relationship, I was aggressive with my approach. I would use loud tones and anger to get my point across. I was communicating, but not effectively. Poor lady! Now, I am more intentional with how I communicate with my wife. I listen and think before I respond. This helps me decide whether a response is necessary. If it is, I reply to educate, enlighten, or explain without expressing resentment.

How you behave toward your lady will impact how she communicates with people, even outside of your home. You can't fake authenticity. Remember when God told Adam to cultivate the garden? He gave that instruction to the man to name the animals, the plants, trees, and all the other living things. God gave you charge to care and to cultivate. Whatever you give a woman, she will multiply it. There's a saying that goes like this:

"You give a woman a house, she makes it a home. You give her groceries and she'll give you a meal. You give her sperm and she'll give you children. You give her words; she'll give you a paragraph!"

-   Unknown

Make sure you treat your wife with the best affection and care you can. How your wife carries herself is a direct reflection of how you treat her. For example, if a man talks down to his wife and doesn't do nice things for her like buy flowers and take her out on dates, she will feel defeated. If she is not strong in her faith in God or is greatly discouraged, she may have an affair to receive kind words, compliments, and kind gestures that her husband doesn't provide.

In the best-selling book *His Needs, Her Needs,* Willard F. Harley, Jr. shares how vital communication is to a marriage. Harley shares stories of infidelity after a spouse ceases to communicate like they used to when they first met.

Make it a habit to make up with your wife when there is tension. Never go to bed angry at each other. I truly believe something happens when we sleep with anger towards one another. Early on in our marriage, I noticed how distant my wife and I got after going to bed upset at one another the night before.

I also discovered I had to at least make things right with my wife even if I wasn't in the wrong. Say something that assures her that you care like, "I understand you are upset, but let's talk about it." Then resolve the conflict. Don't make it a habit to go to bed mad at each other. Share your feelings and disappointment with your lady and allow her to understand your frustration. Talk things through. In these times, with so much temptation and pressure on marriage, you should give your best in your relationship. However, if you are not seeing any positive results in your marriage, please get the help you two need.

Second Component: Connection

Marriage is like two deaths happening so one life can be born.

—   Lionel Hilaire

I never understood why my wife used to tell me that she didn't feel a connection between us. That used to frustrate and annoy me because I wanted to understand what I could do better, but she assumed I knew better. I used to tell her, *"Come here and let's connect!"* It's very easy for us men to be turned on. We oftentimes think connection means sex. All she must do is show up and we're ready! For women, we must take her on a journey in her mind. We must do a series of things to turn her on. It's how they were built.

Like buy her flowers, go out on dates, have conversations with her, and allow her to see and feel that you hear her. Show her affection without signs of wanting sex (hugs, kisses, massages).

Therefore, a man shall leave his father and his mother and hold fast to his wife, and they shall become one flesh.

-    *Genesis 2:24*

Cultivate Means to Pursue

The connection can be lost in marriage if you're not intentional about doing the things you did when you first met her. Every day, you should be winning your wife. It's a lifetime thing. Being comfortable in your union is a very risky thing. In fact, I think it's terrible. It's like saying to your wife, *"Now that I have you, I don't need to work hard to keep you or make our relationship interesting"*. I've made the mistake of coming home after work and going straight to the TV or to bed, paying bills, going to church, and gaining weight; I stopped taking my wife out on dates; I only talked to her about paying bills or the children. I made those things a priority over quality time with my wife.

I didn't show her love with my actions. I had to be intentional with the things I mentioned in the previous paragraph. To be quite honest, I had no clue how to be a husband.

Being comfortable in your marriage is dangerous because it's like a slap in the face to your wife because you are showing her that you are no longer pursuing her. You are no longer interested. When a woman feels her husband is no longer interested, it does something to her self-esteem. Low self-esteem can foster insecurity which makes her accuse you of things you aren't doing. She may accuse you of having an affair. Is she wrong for feeling that way? Maybe, but women are emotional—they tend to lean on their feelings. Make and maintain an intentional connection in your marriage. For an authentic connection to be created in your marriage, you must first have one between God and yourself.

Rain and Bird Poop!

If you two are to become one, connection must be intentional. Tuesday is date night for me and my wife. We like to watch a movie at the theater. If we miss our Tuesday night movie, we may change it to Friday and stay home and watch a movie in the bed. Always remember that there's nothing falling from the sky but rain and bird poop. You must pursue what you want. Connection in your marriage is not going to fall from the sky for you. You have to want it and be intentional.

Plan B

Oftentimes, the connection is lost or does not cultivate properly because we have a *Plan B* in our back pocket. *"If she doesn't act right, I'm gonna make that phone call."*

These were my thoughts and possibly the same thoughts as millions of men. *Plan B is* not always another woman. It could be moving back in with mom or leaving because you want to avoid all the bills and just hang out with *"the boys."*

Men who truly have a desire to make their relationship work and build an authentic connection don't have a Plan B in mind. The only plan is to nurture your marriage. If you want to boost the connection in your marriage, try doing something nice.

Many times, the lack of connection isn't because of how you treat your wife—it could be how you handle finances, your capacity to keep a job, anger issues, and other poor decision making on your part. There must be consistency and stability in your life.

There's no real excuse as to why men gain weight. I used to joke and say I had four children. But really, when my wife ate, I ate! However, if you see that your lady has put on a few pounds (whether it's from giving birth to a child, etc.) you don't necessarily like or that can possibly threaten her health, buy her some tennis shoes, and take her walking or do some activities together to encourage her to drop the unnecessary pounds.

My wife, Sierra, wrote a book called _Ten Keys to Self-Care_. It shares her top ten secrets to help women create life balance and experience emotional freedom. You can find it at SierraHilaire.com. This book is a great guide to helping women:

- Manage stress
- Stop overthinking
- Lose weight
- Balance life

- Find joy
- Feel confident

I recommend my wife's book to your wife because it shows her you care. Applying these principles will surely improve connection in your marriage from your wife's point of view. Sierra receives many great testimonials from women about her book. She understands firsthand how a woman can lose themselves while caring for others. I'm proud to have witnessed my wife become the amazing woman she is today.

Third Component: Comedy

It was the summer of 1999 when my friends were getting in trouble and bringing new friends around that I wasn't too fond of. I had this inner voice that kept telling me that I needed to change, fast. I was around guys that didn't really know what they wanted for their future. All we did was hang out, have sex with girls, beef with guys in our neighborhood, etc. When I also noticed the other guys in my area, I saw how they were smoking weed (sometimes laced weed) and drinking with no real sense of direction. At seventeen, I didn't see myself having a good future if I continued to hang around the guys I was with. I knew something about where I was and where I was headed wasn't right. However, one day, several friends and I were in my parents' backyard just hanging out, goofing around. My older brother was supposed to go on a date, but for some reason, he did not want to go. My brother is an introvert and doesn't like to be put on the spot and does not appreciate people in his business. I believe he declined because he wanted to keep the date a secret.

Me being *Mr. Tough Guy* and a show-off, I said, *"Man, I'll go!"* As I walked to the front, I heard a small voice say, *"Be yourself."* For years, I was always pretending to be someone I wasn't. It began in middle school when I was always ignored, picked on, beat up on, and bullied. I was bullied because I *looked* and *dressed* like a Haitian and because I am of Haitian descent. In my middle school days and beyond, the African American children whose parents were born in the U.S. did not like the Haitian community.

I'm sure they learned this from their parents because I would hear grown adults make hateful remarks toward Haitian people in the grocery store, while driving, etc. Because of this, I felt like I had to become this character people would fear and respect. So when I heard that voice, I immediately pulled my pants up, straightened up my posture, then entered my friend's vehicle. Talk about a bold, bold brother!

Listen, I had nothing to lose up until that point in my life. I was going through depression, uncertainty, low self-worth, and neglect from my dad. Something had to give at this point! What else could go wrong? I had no sense of direction. The people I spent time with were misguided, abandoned, accused, and neglected. I was desperate for a better direction for my life—I had to do something. On the way to my friend's vehicle, I believe it was the Lord's voice that changed my original approach. Acting like a tough guy would have ruined my chances of making a good impression on my new date. I had to be myself... funny.

The very first thing I did in the vehicle was something silly. I don't remember exactly what I did, but all I remember was the first time she smiled at me. We joked and laughed the whole night. It was a night I'll never forget. That night changed the whole trajectory of my life because six years later, I married that woman. I am still that humorous guy she fell in love with.

Yet, it wasn't always this way. For years in our marriage, I buried that funny man. I felt burdened to provide for my family instead of honored.

Working fifty to sixty hours a week put a toll on my mind and body. No one told me that marriage and fatherhood would be so stressful. No one told me not to lose myself, but instead, learn how to work under pressure without allowing it to change who I am. I had to find this out years later, the hard way. I went through deep depression. My home was filled with tension. I didn't like the man I had become.

I realized I wasn't the same Lionel my wife met in that little Toyota Corolla back in 1999. She fell in love with that guy, not this one. Today, I make my wife laugh all the time with jokes, sharing my past, and other silly little things. The steps in this book and the stories I share with you may allow you to grow but remain the man your lady admires as well.

Isn't it weird how we meet a lady, and we are so cool to be around? In the beginning, we make them smile, laugh, feel protected and loved but later, we stop. It's like we get comfortable and feel as if we got what we wanted. My brother, just because this lady agrees to make a commitment and says *"yes"* and *"I do"* does not mean you get to go on vacation and stop being that comical guy she met.

It doesn't matter if you're an introvert. You can still make her laugh and you can make her smile.

Fourth Component: Care

I'm sharing this bonus with you because I think it's essential for you to know. For years, my wife was my mom. She would call all the shots in our relationship. She decided what I should wear, where we should go for dinner, what car to buy, where we should live, eat, etc. My mom raised me while my father worked all day, six days a week. The cultivating I needed from my father never came. He did not show me how to make decisions on my own. He never personally taught me how to care for a family, so I just did what I've always done—received instructions and direction from my wife.

I don't have a problem with women making decisions. I have a problem with it when the man looks like her son. That was me who was still thinking like a boy. I also had very low testosterone levels causing me to experience brain fog, but I had no idea until about ten years later.

One of the major things I did was acknowledge that I needed to go from boy to man. The second thing I did was get help. Help to me was reading books that assisted me to grow into a man and beneficial husband. I read books and watched programs by Myles Munroe, Creflo Dollar, and Stephen Darby, just to name a few.

These men helped me tremendously. Take time to look these men up (especially Stephen Darby on YouTube) and make plans to consume their content. Learn and grow one day at a time. Don't rush because that will only fuel burnout and anxiety. Practice much patience and be okay with what looks like little progress. Remember, caring for your wife begins with you. If you don't properly care for yourself, you can't possibly care for anyone else.

Remember Why

Always remember why you fell in love with your lady. If she becomes ill, take great care of her. When my wife was ill the first time around, I became selfish. I was anxious about my needs. And because of my selfish desires, I had an affair. Mind you, I had no clue that I was broken and behaving selfishly. Later, I discovered the unresolved brokenness from my past surfaced and took over my emotions. The second time she fell ill, I took better care of my wife. I was more mature and had overcome internal challenges. Overcoming lust and brokenness enhanced my attention to my wife. I became her chef and got better at cooking. Now she wants me to cook all the time!

If your wife becomes ill or needs you to step up and do a little more around the house, do it. You may have to wake up earlier to handle the things you need to do for yourself. Do it with honor and gratitude. Who knows, you might become her new chef.

The worst thing you can do is make your lady feel like she is a piece of meat. Paying bills, putting a roof over her head is not enough to turn a mature and confident woman on. Most women crave the experience of foreplay. Foreplay is anything she likes that doesn't require penetration; it is perhaps the most important part of love making. Beyond the bedroom, don't forget what captivated her in the first place. If she expressed to you what made her fall for you, remember that and do it, often. That, too, is a form of foreplay. It shows her that you remember the small things and appreciate her.

That's It?

Brother, if you can get these four steps right, your wife will swear she married a new man and be the happiest woman on the planet. Your lady will feel loved and cared for. She will begin to shine brighter because of the compassion you express towards her.

So, practice *communication, connection, comedy and care* in your marriage and you'll feel like a newlywed.

Here's what you learned in this chapter:

- Make it a habit to make up with your wife when you two have a disagreement. Never go to bed angry at each other.
- Connection in your marriage is not going to fall from the sky. You must want it and be intentional.
- It doesn't matter if you're an introvert. You can make her laugh and smile.
- The worst thing you can do is make your lady feel like she is a piece of meat. Women desire and must experience foreplay.

Communication, connection, comedy, and care (the bonus) are some sure-fire ways to ignite passion in your bedroom. Do these steps with authenticity. Your wife can tell if you're doing it because you have to or because you want to. It's a privilege to serve your lady. Show it.

If you haven't already, I encourage you to buy the book *Ten Keys To Self-Care* by visiting www.SierraHilaire.com. Grab a copy of the book for your wife to read while you're reading this book. With you both reading to better yourselves, it will be a shared journey.

As far as this book, make sure you don't just read through it, but take the steps. Taking steps little by little helps you feel more confident about yourself and your future.

Next, we talk about how to succeed at becoming an effective father, even without having a healthy relationship with your own dad.

Chapter 6

Succeed at Being A Great Father Even Without Having A Healthy Relationship with Your Own Dad

---

Every dad, if he takes time out of his busy life to reflect upon his fatherhood, can learn ways to become an even better dad.

-Jack Baker

And He will turn the hearts of the fathers to their children and the hearts of the hearts of the children to their fathers, lest I come with a decree of utter destruction

-Malachi 4:6 ESV

Glancing back at my life and the lives of my friends and family, I have concluded that the most influential person a boy can have in his life is his father. At thirteen, I had a strong desire for family. That great passion gave me hope to overcome the bullying, neglect, and other trials I was facing in my life. It's like mentally, having a family became the vision and the mission for my life.

This chapter isn't easy for me to write because of the relationship I yearned to have with my father. However, I'm still healing at age thirty-eight from the lost days and times my father and I could've had when I needed him the most. There were moments of regret. Being born to refugee parents from Haiti presented challenges. Life in Haiti was difficult for my parents. All they knew how to do was survive.

For years, my parents were raised under presidents who intentionally kept the people illiterate and in poverty. I like to think my father had it a bit worse. During the times Haitians were migrating to America, my father was a vital resource for Haitians escaping Haiti to hopefully live the American dream. Consequently, one day, my father was caught, arrested, and beaten for weeks until he was unrecognizable.

That didn't deter him or my mom from attempting to escape in the late 70s. My mother went on to learn how to read and write in English. My father didn't. However, he worked hard and made a living like many American-born citizens.

The regrets of not being born to an American dad faded quickly. Those thoughts and emotions are normal to have because they come from pain. I love my dad. The more I comprehend what he's survived, the more I honor him. At age thirteen, I would pretend to be like Levar Burton from *Reading Rainbow*. I would be walking home during school hours because I was just bullied or chased off campus, and I would talk to my audience and say, "Okay, we are here on NW 19th Street and we are going to my house. I'll see you when we get there. We will be right back!"

Here I am, this young boy with hopes and dreams of becoming someone great. Constantly, I would do things like this to take my mind off my hardships. What a great imagination I had. It all began to fade, however, as times became tougher. Weeks, days, and months of being picked on, bullied, and lied on took a toll on me. I was told not to cry because men don't cry. Not knowing how to express my emotions, my behavior began to spiral out of control.

The only time I can recall my dad and I having conversations was when I was in trouble. It really felt like he did all the talking and I just listened. Yep! We were all in the same house, Mom and Dad. My dad had a consistent schedule: work, home, eat, sleep, church, then do it all over again. What I did was the normal thing a boy would do— get in trouble so he can get dad's attention. Thinking back now, my dad would tell me he loved me every time I was in trouble. He never said *I love you son,* outside of that. Naturally, I intentionally got in trouble so my dad and I could talk so he could tell me that he loves me.

Years went by and I became a father at the young age of nineteen. With no real guidance and not being affirmed by my dad, I made plenty of mistakes in my parenting and relationship with Sierra. More children came in the picture, but I was still clueless as to how to be an effective father. I didn't know it at the time, but I had developed some resentment towards my dad and didn't even know it.

Deep down, I was frustrated, angry, and bitter that my dad did not show me how to be a father or husband. I needed him when I was thirteen. Around the age of thirteen is when males make choices in their life when it comes to identity, dreams, visions, etc. This was the case for me during my middle school days. Where was he? Why would he allow those precious days to go by without teaching me how a man walks, talks and how to treat a lady? These were the questions I had. But it was too late. Damage was done in my personal life that later would have an adverse effect on my parenting skills and relationships.

My wife and I have a nonprofit organization, Divine Potential Services Inc. We host events with mental health therapists and other experts. I realized my dad did the best he knew how. I discovered this by listening to the experts we invited to speak at our events. They talked about childhood trauma and other things related to ignorance (lack of knowledge and resources) in African American homes.

If my dad did one thing that was best for me, it was coming to the United States and prevent me from living the life he lived. Wow! I forgave him because I saw that he did what was best for himself and his family. I now understand that his way of loving was normal for him. He expressed his love, although it wasn't the way I wanted it delivered. I love my dad. Our relationship can be better, but I'm grateful for his courage to raise us, even with a traumatic history and no real education.

Like my dad, I've made plenty of mistakes as a father. There are things I've said and done that still sting me until this very day. But I must move on and do my best not to repeat the past. If you can relate to my pain, my hope is that you can move forward by applying these next steps.

3 Actions You Should Take Now to Be an Effective Father

Before I begin, please note that these next set of tips can be implemented with your stepchild(ren), adopted children, nieces, nephews, any minor you have custody of or influence on. Not just your own child(ren). You can also be effective even if you're not living in the home together.

Poverty rates for Black families vary based on the family type. While **23% of all Black families live below** the poverty level, **only 8% of Black married couple families live in poverty,** which is considerably lower than the **37% of Black families headed by single women** who live below the poverty line. The highest poverty rates, **46%,** are for Black families **with children** which are headed by **single Black women**. This is significant considering more than half, **55%, of all Black families with children are headed by single women.**

When I saw these statistics, it was hard for me to continue to write because I know how tough it was for my wife and I to raise children with very little resources and I can only imagine how a single parent must feel. Please read the rest of this chapter with these alarming numbers in mind. I hope this touches your heart and propels you to make plans to be more effective in your home and more active in your community. Thanks in advance.

Action #1: Forgive.

Letting go, let's you go.

- *Allen B. Jackson*

One common thing many men I speak to harbor is unforgiveness. They are finding it hard to forgive their parent(s) for things that happened way back when. Some struggle with how relationships with friends, family, and lovers end. Although we all struggle with these types of issues and more, the one person you need to forgive first is yourself. That's most important. It might be easy to forgive someone else because you may not ever see them again.

But when you must forgive the person that you see every day, you must think of it differently. You see that person in the mirror and in the photos in your phone. You must dress and shower this man. Yeah, him. Buy and say some nice things for him and think positive about him.

The only true way you'll move forward is if you forgive yourself. Accept what you did wrong and the negative self-talk. Not that it makes what you did wrong or right, but you acknowledge and accept that you can't change yesterday.

*If you blame someone else for the
life you have now, you are
admitting that they are the only
one who can fix it.*

- Lionel Hilaire

After you've forgiven yourself, forgive those who hurt you. One of the worst things you can do is carry your pain with you. Holding people hostage in your heart can put wear and tear on your mind and body. It wreaks havoc that you won't realize until it's too late. Resentment is emotionally and mentally damaging. It can ruin your relationships. Holding unforgiveness in your heart also invites demonic spirits into your life. Remember, forgiveness isn't for the other person, it's for you.

Why did I place forgiveness here? Because naturally, people treat others how they treat themselves. It's almost impossible to show unconditional love to your child(ren) with anger and rage inside of you. Oftentimes, we think that we are healed from emotions that force us to act out of character, however, we sometimes transfer those emotions to other areas in our lives—like parenthood. I resented my father for many years. Unforgiveness made me bitter, angry, and frustrated. I expressed those emotions in my parenting without knowing it for many years. Our children need to experience a clean heart. Children need fathers who have been healed from the pain of the past.

One day, I did an audit on my daughters' cell phones. First, I asked all three if they would be honest with me. They all said yes. Little did they know, I had already checked their phones for social media apps I had asked them not to download. They had done it anyway. So, I asked them again, "Can I trust you?" They said yes again.

I was a bit disappointed, but I knew that children require nurturing, cultivation, attention, and guidance. I had already made up my mind that I would forgive them because I understand that it is the love of God, proper correction, and His Word that can change people. Yelling at them will make them feel guilty, rejected, and unloved. As a result, they might seek attention from other people.

After confronting them with what I had found, I simply explained to them that it's very important to be honest. I also shared with them that people would rather you tell them the truth than lie to them. It was a teachable moment for them. I believe they felt corrected, but no loss of love from their father.

You should find healthy and effective ways to communicate with your child(ren). Your approach and forgiveness mean a lot to their mental health, emotional health, and their future. Hurt and broken people oftentimes look for love in all the wrong places. Most broken adults experienced trauma during their childhood days.

When I look at my children, I notice each child has ways about them that remind me of myself. One child has my sneaky ways. Another child has my wild ways. One child has my reserved nature, and the fourth child has my imagination.

I've learned that I can't effectively parent all four the same. One child might learn by me having a simple conversation with them. The other child might need to be grounded. Each child teaches me something about myself. Parenting highlights my strengths and areas I struggle with. Allow yourself teachable moments as a parent.

Action #2: Fun

Your child(ren) might like to dance to music or make videos. A dance video with dad is priceless. How do I know? I've seen dozens of viral dad dance videos. Other videos include dads who take their daughters to the dance, do dance routines, or take their sons to school on his very first day. This also applies to dropping children off at college. Priceless.

Kids are not that picky, at least not as pre-teens. Make the best of the time you have with them. Take plenty of pictures together and smile more often. Have more "no judgment conversations." They need you to be their coach, their cheerleader, and their biggest fan. It's not always the deep-voiced, yelling father who looks over the report card only to criticize the grades he doesn't like. Children desire and need to experience unconditional love and fun with their father.

In my home, "no judgment conversations" are a constant thing, not just occasional. No judgment to me simply means that my children can express how they feel without me taking it personal or being mad at them about what they share with me.

For example, after the death of Tyrell Thrower, my daughter Kyla came to me and asked, *"Dad, how do you know if heaven is for real?"* Long ago, I would've been upset because for many years I took this girl to church and had many conversations about faith in Christ. But I understand that my children must have their own faith in God and have their own experience with Him. Plus, this must have been a challenging experience for an 18-year-old to experience.

I wasn't upset or frustrated. I saw this as a humbling moment for me and a way to step up as a father. I encourage you to have plenty of no judgment conversations with your child(ren). These conversations helped enhance my role as a father. Sometimes my children ask questions I don't know how to answer. When that happens, I do research about the topic so I may have more knowledge in that area and be better equipped to talk about it.

I've learned how to do this without being too serious. I create a balance of fun and education.

Action #3: Family

I don't know all children, but I bet the number one dream of every child is to have and experience a loving home with both parents. If you log on to Facebook and use the hashtag #TheHilaires or #HilaireGirls, you'll see that I took plenty of pictures of my family. When Facebook shows my memories, I text them inside our family group chat to share it with them. We laugh at the missing or crooked teeth, the funny looking hair, and how my wife used to dress our daughters like twins and triplets!

In many of the photos, you might see me in my work uniform. I worked for corporate America and was always working long hours. My eyes were red, and I was just burnt out, but I did my best to be an active dad. The key to an effective family is to be intentional. Life won't ever just hand you time for your family. You have to take it.

Make sure you change things up. Make tacos one week, then make chicken or veggie wraps. The next week, take the family out to eat. If you have multiple children that don't live with you, take them out one by one to their favorite place to eat once or twice per month. Make things interesting. These are memories that help create healthy and mentally strong adults. They will love and adore you for it.

If you have an adult child(ren) you desire to make amends with or have some regrets of being inactive or uninvolved, do the same as I mentioned above. Create memories. Have fun. Apologize with your actions instead of your words.

Give your son and/or daughter valuable advice. Lead by example. Tell them about your childhood. Tell them about an interesting experience that may spark their interest. Always remind them that you love them no matter what they have done. No matter their flaws. Sit and have those moments, where you just look up at the sun or the moon and tell great stories. I love that. I tell my children stories all the time.

My son L.J.—he reminds me of a small version of myself. His imagination is so great. It reminds me of when I was a boy. I enjoy hearing him share stories with me that come from his imagination. I make sure to address imaginations that are not healthy for his growth. For example, he said he is going to kill Coronavirus because he hates being on lockdown. I share with him that he must kill it by taking care of himself by practicing self-care, and I teach him what self-care looks like.

No other word gets me to jump up and move more than the word dad.

I hope you take this all in and apply it. The last two tips not only help children, but they help you feel fresh and full of life. You already have what it takes inside to be the best father and person you can be. You don't have to look externally. Look inside of yourself. Forgive yourself and others. Have fun and be fun to be around. Most of all, make the best of family time. They need you at your best. You are valuable. You are essential. You are necessary. You are significant. I commend you for your efforts in advance.

If you're not a dad yet but desire to be, you have an advantage I didn't have prior to becoming a father. I didn't read a book to address my insecurities or educate myself on how to become a productive father. Take what you've learned and what you know to help empower the men and boys around you.

If you are having a hard time implementing these steps or you would like a one-on-one consultation with me, email me with the subject line *Consultation* at Lionel@lionelhilaire.com.

So, here's what you learned in this chapter:

- The only true way you'll move forward is if you forgive yourself.
- Children want their father's unconditional love and plenty of fun too.
- The key to an effective family is intention. Life won't ever just hand you time for your family. You must make time.

I challenge you to add your children's events to your calendar. Put it on your phone's calendar and make sure you set a reminder. Then talk to your child(ren) and agree to relive that moment together. In the last three chapters, you learned enough to prevent you and your family from going to counseling. I'm not against counseling. I believe it has its purpose. I believe your family can be restored, but that begins with you, not a counselor. The man is the foundation of his home. If he isn't well, the family suffers. Please seek the help you and your family need if things go awry.

In the next section and the closing chapters, I share things you may have overlooked in your life or simply never knew about. I'm excited for you already.

Section Three

Cultivate Your Career & Community

Chapter 7

Discover Your Expertise Without Having Shiny Object Syndrome

The greatest tragedy in life is not death, but life without a purpose.

— Myles Munroe

Myles Munroe is one of the people who made it possible for me to write this book. He helped me dive deeper in discovering my purpose. Dr. Myles Munroe is and will forever be my mentor. He died in 2014, unfortunately, and I never met him in person. The teachings from his YouTube videos and his books have impacted my life greatly. While consuming his content, I fell in love with helping people realize their purpose. A great fire was lit inside of me. As you know by now, I wasn't always this way. In fact, I haven't shared with you one of my deepest and darkest regrets.

I want you to understand why I'm passionate about seeing you succeed in all areas of your life. I am fueled to do what I love and fulfill my calling.

Google defines summons as: *"urgently demand (help)"*

Synonyms: *call for, ask for, request the presence of, demand the presence of, ask, invite, bid*

Early in my marriage, I had no clue what my purpose was. I wasn't thinking about it. All I did was go to work, pay bills, eat, play with my children, and go to bed. This went on for years. At that time, I was irritable. If my wife said something I didn't like, I would pick an argument with her. I hated every minute of it. I always dreamed of having a family of my own, but not like this.

Later, I fell into a deep depression because something just didn't feel right in my life. I felt like a robot doing the same thing over and over. It seemed like there was a dark cloud over my head that wouldn't float away. I had a void inside of me, but I could not explain it. Although I believe nutritional and mental health played a key role in my depression, not understanding my purpose was also a culprit. I lost my desire to properly care for myself.

It was not until 2009 that things began to change. My wife and I were invited to a network marketing presentation at a hotel about residual income, healthy living and self-care. The presentation made me realize I had a closed mind. We joined the company, and I began speaking in front of people, explaining the products and the compensation plan. Life began to improve for me. I loved every minute of it. Right away, I knew that speaking and educating people was a passion of mine. This was the beginning of a journey for me to discover my purpose. All this time, I thought that I needed a degree or traditional education to speak as an expert in front of a crowd, but I did not.

Now it's your turn to discover your purpose. In short, purpose means original intent. You must understand what God's original plan was for you. Read below as I share a few passages of scripture with you.

> *Then God said, "Let us make man in*
> *our image, after our likeness. And let*

them have dominion over the fish of the sea and over the birds of the heavens and over the livestock and over all the earth and over every creeping thing that creeps on the earth."

So, God created man in his own image, in the image of God he created him; male and female he created them. And God blessed them. And God said to them, "Be fruitful and multiply and fill the earth and subdue it and have dominion over the fish of the sea and over the birds of the heavens and over every living thing that moves on the earth."

- *Genesis 1:26-28 (ESV)*

God is a creative Father and He made you in His image after His likeness. That makes you creative also!

Now, let's talk about the things you're good at and passionate about. The best way to complete this is by not answering quickly. Write down your strengths and passions.

Things you're good at

For example, relationships, personal development, marketing, etc.

What advice do others ask you for?

_____

_____

_____

_____

_____

_____

_____

_____

Have you given the same type of advice for free? What is that advice?

_____

_____

_____

_____

_____

_____

What is a topic you can talk about for hours without preparation?

_____

_____

_____

_____

_____

_____

_____

If you were to build a community like a Facebook group with thousands of members, what would you love to share with them?

_____

_____

_____

_____

_____

_____

_____

_____

Great job! Not that bad, right? Let's move on to the next set of questions. Very similar here, except don't give it too much thought. Just write the answers down quickly.

What are five things you are passionate about that make time fly by? For example: fishing, basketball, cooking, bike riding, writing, etc.

_____

_____

_____

_____

_____

_____

_____

_____

Nice! Those were examples of what I enjoy doing. It's like time goes by very fast when I'm doing these things. It puts me in *the zone*. Now, see if your strengths complement what you're passionate about.

For example: I'm passionate about basketball, but I'm not going to try out for the NBA. I'm almost forty, but I might have a gift to coach basketball. I can coach the youth, college, or heck, maybe one day coach in the NBA! Or I can be a consultant to young men who desire to enter the NBA draft. I could give him guidance to make the right decisions.

How do the things you're good at complement what you're passionate about? Write them down and think about how they connect.

Things you're good at

_____

_____
_____
_____

_____
_____

_____

_____

Things you're passionate about

_____

_____

_____

_____

_____

_____

_____

Let's go over something very vital to your journey. It's one of (if not the top) the reasons why entrepreneurs can't seem to get things done. They begin their journey. They work on their expertise. Then the shiny objects get their attention and they rarely, if ever, continue to pursue their calling.

How to Avoid Shiny Object Syndrome (SOS)

The things which are most important don't always scream the loudest.

-   *Bob Hawk*

Speaking, writing, and training are three things I love to do and earn a living while doing so. However, I also like affiliate marketing. Affiliate marketing is selling another person's product to potentially earn a commission. There are good affiliate offers on the market that do very well. The wording in the content and pictures are well thought out and simple to understand. But way too often, I signed up for the flashy offer and made $0.00. The offers that were thoroughly explained to me were the most profitable. I was told expectations, how to use the product, and how to promote the product. These offers weren't flashy, salesy or anything like that. In fact, that was discouraged.

Affiliate marketing is an exploration for entrepreneurs who don't know their purpose or don't have their own product to sell. Affiliates can earn a generous living selling other people's products, but most do not because they do not take the time to learn the basics of the product and offer or jump from product to product, spam accounts or quit prematurely, expecting people to buy just because they're selling it.

Shiny object syndrome (SOS) is not a real medical term, but many people use it to describe potential patterns and toxic behaviors. I use it to get the attention of the person I'm speaking with. To me SOS really is really FOMO: fear of missing out. People fear missing out on what others are receiving or have a fear of failure. However, *"God did not give you the spirit of fear but of power and love and self-control."* 1 Timothy 1:7 (ESV)

Roots

When I speak to family and friends about their careers or what their dreams are, they all seem to have one thing in common. They have gone to college, have thousands of dollars in student loan debt, received one or more degrees and are back in school because they feel like they need *more* education. They jump from career to career, but still feel incomplete; a void is still there.

Their mom or dad told them to become a doctor or a lawyer as the way to a great life. Heck, my mom told me the same thing. Although parents mean well, in our minds we fail if we don't become a doctor or a lawyer. For years, I battled with feeling like I was a nobody because I didn't' live up to my mom's expectations. I went to trade school at age 20 to make my mom proud, but I dropped out because I knew deep down inside that this was not what I enjoyed doing. Years later, I signed up for Phoenix University online to become a firefighter, but I quit because I knew that wasn't for me either. Deep down inside, I felt like I failed her. She thinks graduating from college is what makes a person successful and that if her kids did not graduate, they didn't *"make it."*

One day, I had to politely ask my mom not to mention not "making it" anymore. After I explained how it made me feel when she did, she quickly apologized. She realized how saying it all these years, the body language, the subliminal etc., were hurtful. My mom was born in Haiti. She experienced great poverty and lack. To her, coming to the United States and receiving a college degree is the #1 goal. Knowing that I had not graduated college, that conversation always made me feel a little uncomfortable. When I was twenty, I went to trade school just to impress my mom, but I dropped out because it was just not for me. It felt like I was forced to be someone I was not. Later I learned that it's okay if my mom does not see the vision. It wasn't given to her; it was given to me. I enjoy every moment of inspiring others and utilizing our nonprofit organization as a platform to share my gifts with my community and beyond. The route I'm on got me where I am today, and no one could have drawn this but God Himself! I truly love what I do.

According to the Washington Post, only about 27% of college graduates have a job related to their major. Why is that? Possibly because right after high school, teens feel the pressure to sign up for college even if they're not sure exactly what they want to major in. I'm not against going to college. However, I'm against a person attending college without their own dreams in mind.

To avoid shiny object syndrome, first be aware of the temptation to satisfy the opinions of others. With that, pray. Ask God to guide your steps and lead you to a mentor who has your best interest at heart. Someone who will not simply tell you what you want to hear. Instead, your mentor should challenge you to become the best version of yourself.

Second, make sure whatever you sign up for, read, or are tempted to buy, is in alignment with your goals and your journey. Sometimes we may do the right things, but for the wrong reason. You must count the cost before you commit to anything (Luke 14:28). I suggest you write down your goals and revisit them often. This will help you keep track of your goals and create a plan to achieve them. Pat yourself on the back when you accomplish your goals.

Finally, research and ask questions. Look into that product or service you want to buy or sign up for that can help you. Just because something is free doesn't mean it's worth your time. Time is one thing you cannot get back. Choose wisely.

I wanted to make sure I covered *SOS* with you to help you avoid making the same mistakes I made. Reading the right content and having the proper counsel helps accelerate your success in life and helps you avoid wasted years. Plus, I wanted to prepare you for what I'm about to share with you.

What Has Pained You?

Believe it or not, you know more than you think. I've always been telling folks to turn their pain into gain. It might sound a little weird, but it is worth trying. People have a story behind their success, and it isn't always pretty. Pain is inevitable— you might as well make good use of it.

Did you know that what you went through and overcame is something that somebody is going through right now and will pay you to solve their problem? Yes sir! Think about it. You know a thing or two because you have survived a thing or two, right? Let's go over at least three challenges you overcame. Write the obstacles you have faced and how you pulled through.

First Obstacle

What was the obstacle?

_____

_____

_____

_____

_____

_____

_____

_____

How did you manage to win?

_____

_____

_____

_____

_____

_____

What did you learn from it?

_____

_____

_____

_____

_____

_____

_____

What advice would you give a person who's
going through this obstacle right now?

_____

_____

_____

_____

_____

_____

_____

_____

_____

_____

_____

Second Obstacle

What was the obstacle?

_____

_____

_____

_____

_____

_____

How did you manage to win?

_____

_____

_____

_____

_____

_____

What did you learn from it?

_____

_____

_____

_____

_____

_____

_____

_____

What advice would you give a person who's going through this obstacle right now?

_____

_____

_____

_____

_____

_____

Third Obstacle

What was the obstacle?

_____

_____

_____

_____

_____

_____

_____

How did you manage to win?

_____

_____

_____

_____

_____

_____

_____

What did you learn from it?

_____

_____

_____

_____

_____

_____

_____

What advice would you give a person who's going through this obstacle right now?

_____

_____

_____

Your Past No Longer Matters

Before we go deeper, let me share this with you. It doesn't matter if you dropped out of school, have been to prison, have a felony, are fat, skinny, short, tall, Black, White, or Asian—you can help someone else. You can become an entrepreneur and achieve far more success than you or anyone else could have imagined. Please don't doubt yourself for one minute. Your past is behind you. The windshield is larger than the rear view for a reason. You're supposed to look forward 99% of the time.

In these days and times, you should be looking into entrepreneurship more than ever before. Entrepreneurship allows you to be your own boss and make your own hours. However, entrepreneurship is challenging and takes time to build. There are many tax benefits I'll share later in this chapter. I always advise people to work their 9-5, then work on their business from 5-9. I will also share how you can earn a living sharing your gift and talents with others.

First, I encourage you to imagine yourself winning. Whatever winning looks like to you, just picture it. How much money do you need every month to be able to pay your expenses and save, invest, and spend?

Imagine earning that each month. How would it make you feel to hit your monthly income goals? Now every time you begin to doubt yourself, think about that feeling you had when you imagined how you met your goals. Smile as if it's already done, and it will be.

Premium Only Please!

I'm not saying to hit people across the head with your prices. However, people are willing to pay a premium price to avoid a premium pain. Admit it, just like everyone else (including me), you hate having to go through pain. You only need a few people who need your advice and are willing to pay you for it. I call them your *tribe.*

Let's say you wanted to offer consulting/coaching services. You have about twelve clients per month. This is what you can handle based on your time and experience. That requires three calls or contacts per week. You can handle talking to three people per week for about 1-2 hours per day, right? Okay, just checking. Choose one of the obstacles that you overcame and feel most comfortable giving advice on.

You checked the market and the going rate is $10,000 for twelve weeks (for example) but because you're new to the industry, you offer a lower rate in exchange for written and video testimonials. Your rate is $3,000 for about twelve weeks of your consulting/coaching services.

Grab your calculator to check my math. Okay, $3,000 X 12= $36,000. That's just one quarter. If you decide to keep your price at the lower end because you are passionate about helping others, you will earn $36K per quarter. This equates to $144,000 per year. That is only one stream of income. If you sell books, land speaking engagements, etc., you should be earning more than that. Can you live off $144,000 per year, working at least 6-20 hours per week on average? Just checking again.

Remember, this was just an example. Your tribe might have a lower price point they are willing to pay. If that's the case, if you want to earn at least $144K from one stream of income, just increase the number of clients you serve until your income is $144K or higher. Later, if you decide that you want to give yourself a raise, simply add another stream of income, like writing a book or land paid speaking engagements (in person or virtually). There are so many ways to give yourself a raise. You don't have to wait for your boss to give you that dollar raise you've been asking for all these years.

Your Expertise

You might be saying *"Lionel, I love those numbers, but I don't know what to consult/coach, write, or speak on."* Good thing you brought that up. Here is the last set of questions I want to ask you.

What advice would you have given to yourself 10-15 years ago?

_____

_____

_____

_____

_____

_____

_____

_____

What advice would you give to your daughter about dating?

_____

_____

_____

_____

_____

_____

_____

What legacy should a man leave behind?

_____

_____

_____

_____

_____

_____

_____

_____

Why do you think it's important for a person to discover their purpose?

_____

_____

_____

_____

_____

_____

_____

_____

Why is having a spiritual life and a relationship with God vital?

_____

_____

_____

_____

_____

_____

_____

_____

What would you say is the best way to care for your (mental or physical) health?

_____

_____

What have you learned about wasting time?

The answers to these questions are solutions for your clients. There are people willing to pay a premium price to avoid pain or overcome the pain. Here are seven niches that can be offered as services:

1. Mentoring/Coaching

Tony Robbins is known as the highest paid coach in the world.

2. Dating/Relationships

Do I really have to explain this one? Dating and relationships will always be a hot topic and can be a very profitable one if you are knowledgeable, ethical, and have compassion from others.

3. Real Estate and Investments

Robert Kiyosaki gets paid very well to give advice on this topic. In fact, his book *Rich Dad Poor Dad* sold over 32 million copies in 51 languages. My cousin-in-law Luke Jones started his real estate business and a few years later, it has taken off. You will read more about him towards the end of this book. You can reach out to him for any questions about getting your real estate license. Let him know I sent you. My other friends Jimmie and Arlene Williams also have a very successful real estate investing business and other related businesses. Their information is also towards the end of the book.

Finding and Funding Your Why

Many experts make bank helping people discover their purpose. I am one of them. It's another reason why many men pick up this book. They want to know what they are naturally good at; how to effectively live out their calling and fund it; if they encourage others to discover their purpose or to go after their dreams. I can guide you to become a coach or mentor—contact me today.

4. Spirituality

The Bible is the highest selling book ever. Regular people like Myles Munroe have sold millions of books over the years. Sometimes people publish more than one book per year. Many authors you have never heard of have sold millions of copies as well. However, you don't need to be a big name to become a bestseller. Myles Munroe died years ago, and his books are still selling very well. In fact, I'm going to buy more of his books. The book you write can be used as a business card to help you secure high-paying speaking engagements. Books are a marketing tool, whether you sell them or give them away. You can give books to radio show hosts, bloggers, vloggers, etc. You can also reach out to leaders in communities and organizations that have a platform that might allow you to speak to their audience. Doing so helps you land consulting and coaching clients. Just make sure when you write your book, you let your readers know about your products and/or services.

5. Nutrition, Physical and Mental Health

If you have been around long enough, you have spent a few thousand dollars on one or two of these hot topics. People are being diagnosed with illnesses left and right. So, they want to improve their health. I live in Florida; there have been tragedies, especially in my area. This includes school shootings like at Parkland High School, stabbings, suicides, social media bullying, and much more. Florida is now pumping millions of dollars into the mental health profession. My childhood friend Lucky owns Luck's Fitness. If you are looking to start a fitness business, he is a great person to connect with.

6. Productivity and Time Management

Brendon Burchard is one of the most watched, quoted, and followed personal development trainers in the world. He is a best seller and one of the world's top productivity and time management trainers.

Pain to Profit

Turn your pain into profit. Your tribe is depending on you to help them overcome what has held them back long enough. When you show up in your own life, you inadvertently give inspiration to those whom you didn't even realize were paying attention. You give them someone to look up to and admire to see that their own dreams and desires can come true. When you begin to manage your time, it will appear to others that you're one of the hardest working men they know. Maybe, but more than likely you're working smarter, not harder.

Three ways I manage my time:

1. **Prioritize.** If it doesn't help me reach my goal for the day, it's last or not on my list at all. When I'm working on something that must get done in a short time, I make sure I go to bed earlier than usual.

2. **A planning journal.** I used a journal to plan for this book, and it has helped me

tremendously. A planning journal helps you write your goals, plan your day, then measure your results.

3. **Focus.** With social media, work, and family, it's challenging to be productive. I use a timer to keep track when I am working on something.

Riches Are in The Niches!

The seven topics we just reviewed are called niches. I used to manage a Fortune 500 company. Occasionally, there were problems we couldn't help solve. When that happened, I told the customer to take their vehicle to a specialist. I warned them ahead of time that they would pay a premium price for the service. There were some repairs on cars we could handle, but we had to turn away many vehicles because we were not specialists. Because we lacked the expertise to handle the issues, we made mistakes that required our customers' vehicles to be sent to a specialist. This cost us a lot of money because we had to pay the premium price. We automatically refer certain vehicles and repairs to experts. A niche businessman has the experience, the know-how, and the expertise to handle an area that others do not. He brings in the right team, tools, and skills that are necessary to solve the problem.

We were generalists. We could only charge basic pricing, but a specialist charges a premium price. If you prefer, you can become specialized in a particular subject matter. With advanced training, possibly even furthering your education, you can become an authority that commands premium pricing for your services and/or products.

Don't Pay Taxes!

I'm not literally saying don't pay your taxes. I want you to know that tax laws benefit a person with a w-9 rather than a person with a w-2. As an entrepreneur, if you have employees, provide transportation, housing, or educational services, you can get a tax break. You can deduct almost anything. But as a person with a w-2, you are very limited. Please consult a tax professional to determine your tax breaks and deductions.

Parents receive a tax break, but I'm sure most parents spend more than $2,500 on one child per year. Please do your own research. Taxes for most people are a sensitive subject. I just want you to know that you have options. If you would like to know more about how to legally lower your taxes, I recommend *Tax-Free Wealth* by Tom Wheelwright. He is Robert Kiyosaki's personal Certified Public Accountant (CPA).

Epi That's It!

I love when my Haitian people speak English and Creole at the same time! Epi means *and*. So much in this chapter was covered. I truly hope you love how I over delivered. I think you learned enough to get started.

Here are just a few things you read:

- You were made in the image and after the likeness of God. God gave us dominion.
- To avoid shiny object syndrome, first pray! Ask God to guide your steps and to help you find a mentor who has your best interest in mind and will not simply tell you what you want to hear.

- Use your pain for your gain. Your tribe is depending on you to help them overcome.
- Tax laws were made to benefit the person with a w-9 rather than a person with a w-2.

If you enjoyed what you read in this chapter and would like to start your own business, please email me at Partner@LionelHilaire.com and put *Cultivate Partner* as the subject line. I would be honored to help you serve your tribe and monetize your gift.

Turn the page so we can cover how to influence people and turn your haters into raving fans!

Chapter 8

How to Be Positively Influential Without Showing Off

---

*Do nothing from selfish ambition or
conceit, but in humility count others
more significant than yourselves.*

\-   *Philippians 2:3 (ESV)*

I nearly lost my life when I was a senior in high school (1999-2000). There was a rap label, Cash Money, that was very popular. What really helped them come to great fame was a song they had called *"Bling, Bling."* If you're around my age, you know what I'm talking about. People all over were singing and rapping to this music. If a person knew nothing else, they knew every word to the chorus. *"Bling, Bling."* That's it. I can't tell you how many times I heard that song in a span of two years. The phrase *bling* became so popular, it became a real word and was officially added to the dictionary.

The dress code for these rappers was plain white shirts, baggy blue jeans, Reeboks, expensive cars, and plenty of shiny jewelry on their fingers, wrists, ears and around their necks. I fell in love (lust) with their brand. So much so, I wanted everything I saw they had in the music video. For my senior year of high school, I decided to wear only plain white shirts, baggy blue jeans, Reeboks, and a necklace with a charm all year long just like the Cash Money artists.

The first thing I did was go down to the flea market and put a necklace and a charm on lay-a-way; it all came up to $250. The necklace was the first item I could afford to pay off. I was so anxious to have something to show off! Not working at the time, I begged, cried like a baby, and pleaded for my mom to help me pay off the charm. After some time, she gave in and finally gave me the money. I felt somewhat complete in upgrading my own brand, but I was still riding the school bus. There was no way I was going to miss this one crucial piece of branding, so I asked my dad to buy me a car. A few weeks after submitting my request for help getting a car, my dad came home and said, in his thick Creole accent, *"Lionel! You have to see this car before someone buys it!"* Now I'm thinking this old man knows nothing about the cars I like, so I brush it off. He kept insisting that this was the car for me to buy so to appease him, I gave in. It was December 23rd, 1999 when I saw the car. To my amazement, my dad was right—it was the car I needed to see. When I saw it, I knew immediately that this was the missing piece! The car was a 1994 Pontiac Grand AM, with purple and black crush interior, a black vinyl top with a moonroof, and 17-inch shiny chrome wheels. I was lit with excitement to say the least.

By the time my dad bought the car from me, we were in the second quarter of the school semester. Many of the other juniors and seniors started wearing plain white shirts, baggy blue jeans, Reeboks, and a necklace with a charm because their girlfriends were paying attention to me and that wasn't gonna fly with them. When I arrived at school with my new car, that really set things off. The girls at school would warn me that boys at the school were plotting on taking my necklace. I must admit, I had been in many fights, but I was not truly a fighter. I only fought because I had to. However, I was a big show off and had to prove I wasn't the one any of them wanted to mess with. To prove myself, I stood in the middle of the main hallway and yelled, *"I don't see anybody taking my chain. I wish you would try to take it!"* Not in those exact words, but you get my point. Oh, how I should've never said that...

A few months later, I was jumped and stomped by boys and girls on the north side of the cafeteria. A few of my friends were there to help, but we were outnumbered. It was so bad the school was shut down and the S.W.O.T. was called. At least that's what I heard. I was sent home for ten days. I slept for about seven hours or more due to being stomped on my head. Talk about being beaten to sleep. I may have suffered a concussion but was never diagnosed with one, nor treated for my head injury.

Cash Money had a major influence on me. I had a major influence on the kids at school, but it was negative. It brought out a prideful spirit, anger, jealousy, envy, and hate. So much so, I almost lost my life. I was kicked out of high school when I attempted to return after the suspension.

Years later, the Cash Money team separated. A few of the younger rappers did ten or more years in prison. One is currently serving time as I write this book. Another one looks drawn up like he is very old and sick, but he is my age. But the two men who founded the group appear to be doing just fine. These men had the chance to influence these boys they were mentoring in a positive way, but they took another route. The boys are men now, but their lives will never be the same.

When I was a child, I spoke like a
child, I thought like a child, I
reasoned like a child. When I became
a man, I gave up childish ways.

-1 Corinthians 13:11

To this day, men around 40 to 50 years old, continue to carry on like boys. Cash Money rappers were not my only influence, but I use them as an example because they helped shift rap music and life in such a way that Webster and Google bought into it and placed the word *bling* in the dictionary and on Google!

Show off The Right Way

I consider myself an extrovert. Extroverts are usually outgoing, and we love company. I used to show off so much, I was usually the center of attention. Doing this in front of friends and others gave me a temporary high. Some people loved me while others hated me. Being this way can be both a gift and a curse if you don't learn how to conduct yourself and use wisdom. I experienced a few burnouts, nervous breakdowns, and panic attacks due to using my energy to show off. Burnout helped me mature and recognize what's meaningful. I learned peace, gratitude, respectability, and how to treat others well.

After reading this book, you have two options. You can take what you learned and take advantage of people, ruin lives, show off your nice cars, jewelry, and other material things. Or you can take everything you have learned and bring young males under your wing to show them the right way a man should conduct himself. You can also put these teachings to use by protecting our women and children, give to nonprofit organizations, serve your city and over-deliver in everything you do. That's the right way to show off. Show Satan that what he meant for wrong, God allowed you to make right. You and those you were called to serve will benefit from your righteousness.

God took you in while you were broken. He molded you the way He saw best. Show up and show out the right way...God's way.

Be Perfect

*For everyone who exalts himself will
be humbled, and he who humbles
himself will be exalted.*

—   Luke 14:11

When someone mentions you now, let it be about your humility, the compassion you show your community, and how you correct your mistakes. Let your service be great. Never allow awards and accolades to change you. Put them next to the photos of the people you were called to serve.

I have served in positions at work and in ministry for many years, and I have seen more than enough to discern when someone leads with pride or humility. In the same manner, people around you can discern if you're being authentic or artificial. It's very hard to hide unnatural ways, trust me. So be your new self. The one who is in Christ.

*Therefore if any man [be] in Christ,
[he is] a new creature: old things are*

passed away; behold, all things are become new.

- *2 Corinthians 5:17*

<u>Unlearn</u>

Half of wisdom is learning what to unlearn.

- *Larry Niven*

Many people are big on learning new things and often encourage others to do the same. They take advice, buy books, programs, and have several mentors. That's all good and everything, but sometimes unlearning is just as effective as learning.

And no one puts new wine into old wineskins. If he does, the wine will burst the skins—and the wine is destroyed, and so are the skins. But new wine is for fresh wineskins.

-Mark 2:22 (ESV)

Learning new things without unlearning bad habits is pointless. After playing basketball and getting all sweaty, would you put on a clean suit afterwards? I hope not. Disgusting, right? So many of us do that when it comes to knowledge. We may recognize we have an issue; we quickly learn how to solve it but neglect to denounce it. We must denounce and prevent the dog mentality.

Have you ever seen two people living together and one person is very neat, yet the other person is very sloppy? Sooner or later, somebody has to go or sooner or later, someone is going to give in. They just don't mix. If the spirit of pride isn't condemned before you serve others, it may take over and cause you to do great harm to yourself and the people around you. Denounce the seduction of pride every time it arises.

I have great hopes that you will make the right decision and serve in greatness. After all you've been through, I'm sure that you don't plan to go back and relive those deep and dark days. I speak life and blessings over you right now. I speak that no weapons formed against you shall prosper and that you will win in all areas of your life starting today!

Wrap It Up

Another chapter wrapped up. However, please revisit this chapter as you grow in your gift. Allow it and the Holy Bible to increase your effectiveness and humility.

In chapter 9, I will explain how to do it even if you're afraid. But first, here is what we covered in this chapter:

- Show Satan that what he meant for wrong, God allowed you to make right.
- Never allow awards and accolades to change you.
- Denounce the seduction of pride every time it arises.

What did you like best about this chapter? Please share it with me. I want to know. Share by posting a line or two and tag me on social media. I'll be glad to read what you liked best. Thanks!

Chapter 9

Become The "Go to Guy"... Even If You Have Some Self Doubt!

Leadership Synonyms

Guidance, Direction, Initiative, Government, Authority, Management

Each word above represents characteristics you should possess if you want to live in your purpose because that is the call on a man's life. A man is supposed to guide those under his care. Oftentimes, you may have to take the initiative when things need to get done.

Give direction to prevent missteps. Advise men and women so they can help make your community an effective place to live, work, and play. Walk and speak in authority when the enemy attempts to threaten your domain.

The "*Go to Guy*"

In April 2011, I was hired to work full-time at a Fortune 500 company. This was after working odd jobs on and off part-time for nearly two years with a family to provide for. I was in a very low place at the time and there were many days I was hoping that my landlord didn't evict us. Although my bills reflected that I needed a six-figure salary, my employer paid me $8 per hour. I had no other job offer. I remember grabbing a calculator and trying to figure out how we were going to come out of debt because we were five months behind on our rent!

My wife saw me calculating and punching the numbers and she said something like, *"Don't worry about that. God is going to take care of it. You just do your part and work."* Her words of encouragement lifted a gorilla off my back and gave me the confidence to move forward. She reminded me that God was in control. Although I had years of management experience under my belt, I knew all I needed was a fresh start. I would do my best to provide for my family.

Two months later, the assistant manager called me to the front office. He said, *"You don't belong back there. I'm going to promote you and send you to a store."* I was thrilled to say the least! I made a step toward better providing for my growing family. For nearly three years, I worked very hard to provide for my family. I took a $16,640 annual salary and turned it into a $40,000 annual salary! This brother worked hard, man.

In 2014, after seeking a promotion several times, while working under corrupt leadership, I was finally promoted to assistant manager. I heard voices telling me that I wasn't ready and that I'm not good enough. But the thoughts about my family superseded the voices, and it overpowered my self-doubt. Of course, I didn't qualify for the position given I was a high school and college dropout applying for a position that required a college degree. I landed that position. There was a plan in place for the store to be closed and moved a few miles down the road. My manager came to me and said, *"The increase in revenue and traffic has forced us to make the decision to not close down and move. We will remain here and remodel. This location will be the first in the county to be remodeled and corporate execs will travel down just to see this location when the renovation is complete!"*

Two months later, my store manager said, *"Lionel, I am being promoted and because of that, I am giving you the store."* *I was* the new store manager. Store manager wasn't on my mind. All I wanted to do was provide for my family. I didn't care that I didn't qualify. I knew that my heart was in the right place. Talk about double promotion. Not long after, I became the *go to guy* in my community. I served the people with compassion. I knew the customers by name. Heck, I even knew some phone numbers by heart. That's how connected I was with my customers. They would send their family and friends with no problem because I was able to gain their trust and business. If you want to be the guy people recommend, you must serve with integrity and compassion.

Some people claim they specialize in marketing. I say that you must specialize in relationship marketing. Build a relationship first; it doesn't matter if it's on your job or in your business. Even if you are being pressured by the sales numbers, you must develop trust. There's a saying that goes, *"People buy from those they know, like, and trust."* You cannot fake great customer service. Your customers can see right through it.

Born Again

Therefore, if anyone is in Christ, he is a new creation. The old has passed away; behold, the new has come. 18 All this is from God, who through Christ reconciled us to himself and gave us the ministry of reconciliation; 19 that is, in Christ God was reconciling the world to himself, not counting their trespasses against them, and entrusting to us the message of reconciliation. 20 Therefore, we are ambassadors for Christ, God making his appeal through us. We implore you on behalf of Christ, be reconciled to God. 21 For our sake he made him to be sin who knew no sin, so that in him we might become the righteousness of God.

-2 Corinthians 5:17-21

The world will always remember the things you have done wrong. You must pay by serving time in jail, paying fines and/or have a record tied to your social security number for life. But in Christ, you are forgiven, and your trespasses are not counted against you. But you must also not count them against yourself because that was the old you. Now you are a new man.

If anyone from your past claims they know you, tell them that man died a long time ago. If anyone brings up your history, say "I don't recall." Do not let anyone resurrect that old man (including you). Keep him buried. This means do not conduct yourself in your old ways. Leave pride, anger, fornication, heavy partying, drunkenness, homosexuality, lust, greed, and other ungodly ways behind.

Recreate your environment if necessary. Belief in yourself won't just happen. It's not going to fall from the sky. *"There's nothing falling from the sky but rain and bird poop."* You must create the life and environment you want and deserve without *E.G.O.* -Edging God Out. Keep God at the center of all your decision making. Yes, you will make mistakes; that is okay. Get that part straight with yourself. People will think you're crazy to live your dreams. Remember your dreams were given to you, not them. The obstacles that you face prepare you for your greatest self and best life.

<u>You Have Enough, You Have Him</u>

And he said unto me, My grace is
sufficient for thee: for my strength is
made perfect in weakness.

-      *2 Corinthians 12:9 (KJV)*

Trauma can stop you from moving onward. You will have days where you ask, *"Why me?"* There will be times when God gives you this great feeling to step out on faith and start a movement or increase your reach, but fear says, *"It's too much. It's bigger than me. What will people think? I'm insufficient."* But God says, **"My grace is sufficient!"**

When you attempt to do things your way and don't allow God to lead and guide you, you will always feel insufficient.

-      *Lionel Hilaire*

Occasionally, we can get in our own way. Ask yourself who you are doing this for, yourself or God? Remember that you are His messenger. God placed you here so He can speak and work through you. He has also allowed people to be around you so their gifts can complement yours and vice versa. You are not alone on this journey.

If You Do It for The Money, You Won't Make Any

> *No one can serve two masters, for either he will hate the one and love the other, or he will be devoted to the one and despise the other. You cannot serve God and money.*
>
> - *Matthew 6:24 ESV*

For years, I've been calling myself a *paper chaser.* I was right—money just kept running away from me. You must have a vision for your future. Ask yourself, *What change do I want to see?* Have a driven mission statement that explains why your movement exists in the first place. Money is a byproduct of the success of your vision and mission. Make sure you write them both down and review them daily.

You must place service before money. One day I met a guy who said his number one goal in life was to make a million dollars, but when he made a million dollars, he was still broken and felt unfulfilled. We talked for nearly two hours during which he revealed his passion for saving animals and helping people in need. His problem was that he didn't know how to practice healthy boundaries. He didn't know how to say no to people. I advised him to purchase my first book that shares what boundaries are and how to set healthy boundaries. He allowed people to run over him. I was inspired by his story because I felt his compassion and energy through the phone. It was as if this man became transformed at that moment. He said the instant he wanted to change his life, I came into the picture and he was so grateful I did. I'm grateful that I had the chance to help him. He has a resource that can help change lives. He must commit to the Source so he can give and serve in a healthy way, or he will harm himself and others along the way.

You never know who you're going to meet. Be ready and confident. Do it afraid. Move with uncertainty. Resist the pressure. Self-doubt will never go away; it will always be there to some degree. Keep going as you rest, restore, and restart your journey.

Have fun along the way and get the rest you need so you can be effective. The more you neglect yourself, the louder the voices get. But the better you care for yourself, the quieter those voices become. Understand how the enemy works. He enters a home through the smallest cracks. Seal all the cracks and secure your home, because he will make his way in if you don't.

Odds & Statistics

Years ago (age 23) when I was working for a major retail company, a manager position became available. I applied for it after someone told me that it would be the first time a black person retained the position. I knew the odds were doubled against me, but because I'm competitive, I applied anyway. Boom! I landed the position. However, a few people didn't like that. I went through some really hard times as my supervisor's boss would nitpick every little thing. He made racial comments towards me as well. One day he said, *"If it were a basketball, you'd know how to do this easily."* This man hated me being in the role. My supervisor used to tell me he doesn't know why this man treated me the way he did, but I knew why... my skin color.

The greater the things you attempt to accomplish in your life, the more odds will be stacked against you. If you're African American, you more than likely have double the odds against you. It's okay. You have my support. Don't run back to your comfort zone. If you want to be your own boss, learn a new skill, then build by monetizing that skill. Don't leave your job until you are satisfied that your income can support you and your family. Find a mentor for each area of your life. Overcome odds by leveraging relationships. Remember, odds will be stacked up against you and that's okay.

Take great care of your mental health, physical health, family, and your finances. No one should know more about these areas than you. You must master your life according to God's word. I call it *existence mastery*. If you are having doubts about yourself, that's okay. Do it with doubt. Do it afraid. Recreate your environment. Many say you become like the five people you spend the most time with. This means you must evaluate your surroundings. Make some changes if you must.

It's About That Time

My brother, you have two choices. You can go with the flow of life, or you can take life by the horns and recreate your world. What I have shared with you in this book is just a snippet, but enough to get you off to a fresh start. I hope you join me to help males become effective men, fathers, husbands, and leaders in our communities. Let's partner up and crush the adversities that are piled up mountain high against us. Let's make our world a better place to live, work, and play. Let's cultivate the call on our lives.

You have what it takes. You don't have to guess or ask around; you possess greatness on the inside of you. Everything you need to launch has already been given to you by God. You are enough. We all struggle with insecurities—don't let those insecurities stop you.

Sow your seed in the morning, and at evening let your hands not be idle, for you do not know which will succeed, whether this or that, or whether both will do equally well. -Ecclesiastes 11:6.

In other words, go to your 9-5, then work your 5-9. Work on your gift after work. Your tribe needs you. If you don't step up to the call, they might fall by the wayside. *You're not called to the world, but you're called to your world.* Your world meaning the people that are within your reach— on or offline. The people you were called to serve need you to cultivate your gift. Learn about it. Use it. Refine it. Leverage your resources and give it your all. Lay it all out on the table every day. Balance your everyday life. Don't forget to rest. I'm here for you—rooting and cheering. Let's make this world a better place. I believe you can... but you MUST believe...

Your #1 supporter,

Lionel Hilaire

PS—always remember, *"There's nothing falling from the sky but rain and bird poop. You have to take your success."* #LionelSpeaks

Sponsors!

Special Thanks to Our Major Sponsors!

These sponsors made it possible for this book to be published without any financial hurdles. From the bottom of my heart, I thank all of you. Please review our sponsors' information. If you or someone you know can use their services, give them a call, thank them for their sponsorship, and patronize their businesses. Thanks in advance!

JW Acquisitions and Development

A Little Bit About Us:

After personally starting about 50 companies and working nearly 50 jobs, my wife and I finally found success when we dedicated our lives to pouring our knowledge, time, and expertise into the lives of others. We had no idea that our businesses would transform at the rate it has, and it's all due to the glory and power of the Most High Yah (God).

Vision and Mission Statement:

We are dedicated to empowering African American, minority & low-income communities with financial education in the areas of real estate and business development. We've helped over 50 Companies achieve economic success. Additionally, we have assisted over 500 Students globally with personal development, so they are well equipped with the right mindset and tools for success.

<u>Our Online Presence (Website and Social Media Platforms)</u>

Website:
https://jwacquisitionsanddevelopment.com/

Instagram:

https://www.instagram.com/jwacademycoach

Twitter:

https://twitter.com/JWAcademyCoach

YouTube Channel:

https://www.youtube.com/channel/UCwdBXDB8gJtLyZGis-tBjlw/featured

Facebook Public Figure Coaching/Mentoring Page (Real Estate/Personal Development)

https://www.facebook.com/JimmieWilliamsRealEstateCoachMasterMentor/

Facebook Real Estate Group:

https://www.facebook.com/groups/JWAcquisitionsandDevelopment

Jimmie Williams

Phone: 404-720-9034

Email:
Admin@jwacquisitionsanddevelopment.com

Address: <u>400 W Peachtree St (Suite #4), Atlanta GA 30308</u>

Office Hours: 10:00am - 5pm EST (Please leave a message if you miss us!)

UR Deziin Inc.

A Little Bit About Us:

After helping my hubby start numerous companies and working numerous jobs, we noticed we gained experience in marketing, branding, and reputation management and saw the importance of it. However, we never realized that God would bring us to this point just because we wanted to give others a platform that we never had.

Vision and Mission Statement:

At URDezign, we're here to help your business stand for something people believe in. An identity you want to assume, a team to suit up for, a tribe where you belong. When your business values are authentic, energizing, and shared by your company, employees, and customers, you have a marketing strategy that everyone buys into. We bring key components together to give you the whole business package. We are changing the world, one business at a time.

Our Online Presence

Website: https://urdeziinevolution.com/

Instagram:
https://www.instagram.com/ur_deziin/

Facebook Public Figure Coaching/Mentoring Page (Strategic Brand Coach)

https://www.facebook.com/URDeziin/

Please feel free to make an appointment to discuss your business here:

3343 Peachtree Road. (St# 180 – 1515)

Atlanta, GA 30326

Business Line: 470. 441. 0917

"Changing the world, One design at a time."

\-   *Arlene Williams*

Jones Luxury Real Estate Group

Luke Jones
Our vision is to shine a light on the pathway to the American Dream.
FB: @JonesLuxuryRealEstateGroup
IG: @YourBrokerLukeJones

About the Author

My name is Lionel Hilaire, and I am Cofounder of Divine Potential Services, where we help restore families and empower change in our community.

I'm a published author, speaker, and consultant but most importantly, I am a husband to Sierra and father to Kyla, Chelsea, Syleena, and Lionel Jr. Hilaire.

My mission is to get a copy of this much needed, overdue book in the hands of 100,000 Black men so our homes and communities become better places for men, women, and children to live, work, and play.

www.ingramcontent.com/pod-product-compliance
Lightning Source LLC
LaVergne TN
LVHW051050080426
835508LV00019B/1798